Zenoss Core Netwo
System Monitoring

A step-by-step guide to configuring, using, and adapting
the free open-source network monitoring system

Michael Badger

BIRMINGHAM - MUMBAI

Zenoss Core Network and System Monitoring

First published: June 2008

Production Reference: 1060608

Published by Packt Publishing Ltd.
32 Lincoln Road
Olton
Birmingham, B27 6PA, UK.

ISBN 978-1-847194-28-2

www.packtpub.com

Cover Image by Nilesh R. Mohite (nilpreet2000@yahoo.co.in)

Credits

Author

Michael Badger

Reviewers

Mark Turner

Matt Ray

Mark Hinkle

Erik Dahl

Acquisition Editor

Bansari Barot

Technical Editor

Usha Iyer

Editorial Team Leader

Akshara Aware

Project Manager

Abhijeet Deobhakta

Project Coordinator

Zenab Kapasi

Indexer

Monica Ajmera

Proofreader

Camille Guy

Production Coordinator

Shantanu Zagade

Cover Work

Shantanu Zagade

Foreword

As the world becomes more connected, the complexity of information technology is expanding. Information workers rely on an expanding number of technologies to collaborate: email, instant messaging, web forums, and wikis. Organizations that at one time relied solely on paper are becoming more dependent on information systems. In addition there is an increase in network-enabled devices including security systems, building environmental controls, power meters, and more. IT administrative staffers are responsible for a growing number of services and the IT fabric used by organizations is continuing to become more intricate.

The way we develop technology is also changing. Highly skilled programmers once wrote their code secretly behind closed doors. This is the old way of doing things Today millions of people develop, distribute, and use open-source software that is produced collaboratively over the Internet. The new model thrives on user input and collaboration. It enables the users of software to take control and become produces of technology the barrier for participation has been lowered.

The trends of open source software use and a growing complexity in information technology have lead to the perfect storm for the adoption of open source systems management. It's no longer good enough to have tools that are purpose-built. It's just as important to have management tools that are easy to deploy, easy to use, and easy to integrate with existing systems. This presents an opportunity for system and network administrators to deploy open source systems management tools that can be adapted to an ever-changing environment.

Zenoss Core was developed to be both adaptable and scalable yet easy enough for even the smallest organizations to use. Released under the GNU Public License (version 2.0) Zenoss has been downloaded over 500,000 times and used by thousands of IT professionals every day to monitor and manage IT infrastructure. The Zenoss community that supports and contributes to Zenoss has grown to over 33,000 members who consistently help improve and expand Zenoss' capabilities.

The open-source development and distribution model is the key factor that allows users of the software to have full access, not just to run the program, but also to modify and redistribute it. This freedom is one reason that Zenoss' popularity has risen so quickly. Zenoss Core presents a unique opportunity for systems management professionals, as it is enterprise-grade software but also free and open source.

In true open-source fashion, this book was not written by Zenoss project members or Zenoss Inc. employees. It was authored by one of our community members who was passionate about our software and took it upon himself to share his knowledge. We are very proud that our software generates that kind of enthusiasm and hope that our efforts and the efforts of our community of users are evident as you use Zenoss Core.

Mark R. Hinkle
VP of Community Zenoss Inc.
`http://community.zenoss.com`

About the Author

Michael Badger is a technical writer with a BS in Technical and Professional Communication from the Pennsylvania College of Technology/Penn State. He has been helping users understand, troubleshoot, and use technology for the better part of 15 years. In the 1990's, he rose through the ranks at the industry leading internet service provider, MindSpring, to manage a technical support call center in Dallas, TX. He later found himself supporting and writing about Win4Lin, a Windows virtualization solution for Linux. Today, he prefers to fill a generalist's role with a focus on automated web application testing and writing—always looking to learn the next cool application or technology. For fun, he prefers to be outside in the wilds of Central Pennsylvania fishing, hiking, and hunting.

Acknowledgement

I'd like to thank Mark Hinkle for connecting me with Packt Publishing and helping me get this book started. You believe in my writing and my work ethic, and for that, I can only say thank you. I am honored to call you my friend.

Thank you, Zenoss, Inc., for providing me with support in the way of training and resources. Chet Luther, your superb training and support accelerated my Zenoss learning curve dramatically. Thank you, Drew Bray, for providing some documentation to help me get started in my research.

Bill Karpovich and Erik Dahl, I enjoyed our conversations. Of course, without Erik I wouldn't have a software application to write about. Thank you.

I owe a special thank you to my primary reviewers, Mark Turner and Kells Kearney. I appreciate every last comment you provided to me, and have no doubt that your work has improved the quality of this book. Mark, it has been a pleasure to work with you again, and I hope that we can collaborate on future projects. Kells, thank you for accepting my invitation to review, and I look forward to working with you in the future.

I'd like to thank my writing mentor, Charles Kemnitz, for preparing me to write my first book. Your guidance and disciplined advice gave me the confidence to know that once I started writing, I would finish.

Christie, my dear wife, I owe you so much. Perhaps there were better times to write a book, but now is my opportunity. You encouraged me to take it. Now we can pause to take an inventory of our accomplishments: We're settled in a new house, we finished the baby's room, Cameron was born, and I wrote a book. I'd say that was a productive six months.

About the Reviewer

Mark Turner has worked with open source since 1994 in IT management, sales engineering, and client services roles. His focus has been on Linux, asterisk, OpenLDAP, and network management solutions. His last role was with Zenoss as a client services engineer where he provided consulting, support, and training for Zenoss customers.

Table of Contents

Preface

Regardless of the size of your organization, information technology (IT) plays an increasingly important role in day-to-day business, which implies we have incentives to manage the servers, routers, workstations, printers, and other systems attached to our networks. *Zenoss Core Network and System Monitoring: A Step-by-Step Guide for Beginners* provides a narrowly focused guide that helps users set up an environment to manage their IT assets regardless of systems administration background or lack thereof.

We use step-by-step examples with ample screen captures to demonstrate Zenoss Core's capabilities that you can easily apply to your environment. The book keeps the emphasis on using Zenoss Core through its web interface. Advanced users will be able to identify ways in which they can customize the system to do more, while less advanced users will appreciate the ease of use Zenoss provides.

If you work through each chapter in sequence, you will start with installation and finish with monitoring solution that can be deployed on your network. Each chapter builds on the knowledge gained from the previous chapter. However, each chapter can stand on its own, allowing you to pick and choose the features you want to explore.

What This Book Covers

Chapter 1 – Introduction: Provides an overview of Zenoss Core's network and systems management capabilities.

Chapter 2 – System Architecture: Discusses the underlying components and how they fit together to form Zenoss Core.

Chapter 3 – Installation and Setup: Details step-by-step instructions for each of the three installation methods—As a virtual appliance, from a binary installer, or compiled from source. Information on how to prepare servers to be monitored is also covered.

Chapter 4 – Zenoss Dashboard: Introduces the web interface's navigation and organization properties. The dashboard holds the key to the rest of the book. From Chapter 4 onwards, the emphasis is on using the dashboard.

Chapter 5 – Device Management: Walks through the process of discovering and modeling devices to build an inventory of the network. In Zenoss, everything is viewed as a device, and without devices, we have nothing to monitor.

Chapter 6 – Status and Performance Monitors: Describes how to set up monitoring so that we know the operational status of our devices and components, such as file systems, interfaces, and processes.

Chapter 7 – Event Management: Provides an in-depth review of how Zenoss Core generates events and how we can manage them from the Event Console.

Chapter 8 – System Reports: Takes us on a tour of Zenoss Core's included reporting features. The reports aggregate system-wide data to provide real-time and historical status views about devices, events, and performance.

Chapter 9 – Settings and Administration: Documents how to manage users, define alerting rules, and customize event views. Includes information about general Zenoss Core administration, including backups and updates.

Chapter 10 – Extend Zenoss: Extend Zenoss Core with ZenPacks, Nagios plugins, and command line utilities.

Chapter 11 – Technical Support: The place to start when things go wrong. Outlines the vibrant community support resources and provides a synopsis of how to troubleshoot Zenoss Core.

Appendix A – Event Attributes: A table of available event fields that are used to describe and process events.

Appendix B – TALES and Device Attributes: Provides a list of the device and event attributes available to the Templating Attribute Language Expression Syntax (TALES).

What You Need for This Book

Hardware

Actual server specifications may very depending on the amount and frequency of the data you collect. Zenoss Inc. recommends the following hardware specifications for a production monitoring server:

- Network with up to 250 devices
    - ◦ 4 GB RAM
    - ◦ Core 2 Duo E6300 1.86/1066 RTL
    - ◦ 75 GB disk storage

- Network with more than 250 devices
    - ◦ 8 GB RAM
    - ◦ XEON 5120 DC 1.86/1066/4MB
    - ◦ Four 75 GB drives in two RAID-1 pairs

The following table shows the available installation options.

Installation Type	Platform
Virtual Appliance	Windows
	Linux
Binary Installer	Red Hat Enterprise Linux 5
	Fedora Core 6
	SUSE
Source	Ubuntu
	FreeBSD
	Solaris 10
	Mac 0S X
	Other Linux environments

Virtual appliance users do not need to install any dependencies because they are included in the image. For all other installations, you need to install the following software packages prior to installing Zenoss:

- MySQL 5.0.22 or higher
- MySQL development environment
- Python 2.3.5 or 2.4
- Python development environment

If you plan to build a Zenoss installation from source code, you need to install the following:

- SWIG
- Autoconf
- GNU build environment

We also need SNMP.

Who Is This Book For

This book is for anyone who would like to proactively monitor their network resource, including Windows and Linux systems administrators.

Readers should have a basic knowledge of networking concepts and be able to administer the systems they plan to monitor. Some Linux knowledge is helpful but not required. This book does not assume any existing system and network monitoring experience.

Conventions

In this book, you will find a number of styles of text that distinguish between different kinds of information. Here are some examples of these styles, and an explanation of their meaning.

Code words in text are shown as follows: "We can include other contexts through the use of the include directive.'

A block of code will be set as follows:

```
#Setup Zenoss environment
export ZENHOME=/usr/local/zenoss
export PYTHONPATH=$ZENHOME/lib/python
export PATH=$ZENHOME/bin:$PATH
```

Any command-line input and output is written as follows:

```
zentestcommand --device=Fox –datasource=checkCpu
```

New terms and **important words** are introduced in a bold-type font. Words that you see on the screen, in menus or dialog boxes for example, appear in our text like this: "clicking the **Next** button moves you to the next screen'.

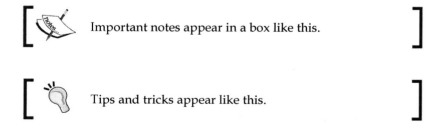

Important notes appear in a box like this.

Tips and tricks appear like this.

Reader Feedback

Feedback from our readers is always welcome. Let us know what you think about this book, what you liked or may have disliked. Reader feedback is important for us to develop titles that you really get the most out of.

To send us general feedback, simply drop an email to feedback@packtpub.com, making sure to mention the book title in the subject of your message.

If there is a book that you need and would like to see us publish, please send us a note in the **SUGGEST A TITLE** form on www.packtpub.com or email suggest@packtpub.com.

If there is a topic that you have expertise in and you are interested in either writing or contributing to a book, see our author guide on www.packtpub.com/authors.

Customer Support

Now that you are the proud owner of a Packt book, we have a number of things to help you to get the most from your purchase.

Downloading the Example Code for the Book

Visit http://www.packtpub.com/files/code/4282_Code.zip to directly download the example code.

The downloadable files contain instructions on how to use them.

Errata

Although we have taken every care to ensure the accuracy of our contents, mistakes do happen. If you find a mistake in one of our books—maybe a mistake in text or code—we would be grateful if you would report this to us. By doing this, you can save other readers from frustration, and help to improve subsequent versions of this book. If you find any errata, report them by visiting http://www.packtpub.com/support, selecting your book, clicking on the **let us know** link, and entering the details of your errata. Once your errata are verified, your submission will be accepted and the errata are added to the list of existing errata. The existing errata can be viewed by selecting your title from http://www.packtpub.com/support.

Questions

You can contact us at questions@packtpub.com if you are having a problem with some aspect of the book, and we will do our best to address it.

1
Introduction

If you have ever arrived at work to answer voice mails and emails about a down web server, print server, or mail server, then you must be familiar with the customer-driven monitoring solution. It's cheap to implement but unreliable, and sometimes the monitor gets an attitude and for good reason. Our customers should not bear the responsibility of monitoring our networks for problems. Unfortunately, commercial monitoring tools lie beyond the budget of many organizations, and the available open-source tools require several packages to be "glued" together by users to get a complete solution.

Zenoss Core replaces prohibitive costs and incomplete solutions with a capable, feature-rich network and systems monitoring package.

What is Zenoss?

Zenoss Core challenges the systems-monitoring landscape with an open-source enterprise management solution that provides a single, web-based point of access to configure, manage, monitor, and report on our IT assets. We get a "single pane of glass" view of our IT assets including routers, servers, and environment. With Zenoss, the question changes from, "Should I monitor my IT resources?" to "How can I afford not to monitor my network?"

Zenoss Core is a web-based application which installs to a central server on the network and uses the Zope application server. It is written in Python. It's a Linux-based application, but we do not need to be Linux administrators to install and use Zenoss Core. Zenoss Inc. releases a virtual appliance that requires no Linux knowledge or setup and enables Mac, Windows, and Linux users to install Zenoss Core inside VMware Player or VMware Server.

The Zenoss Core native Linux installers continue to improve and support a broader range of distributions, which means the Linux skills required to install Zenoss Core natively continue to decrease. Starting with the Zenoss Core 2.2 release, we will have the option of using point and click installers built on BitRock installers; but don't worry, we can still install from source if we so choose. Chapter 3 outlines several installation options.

Administrators access Zenoss Core via a web interface that allows us to do:

- Device Management
- Availability and Performance Monitoring
- Event Management
- System Reports Generation
- User and Alert Management

We can do all this from a web portal, which we will look at first.

Web Portal

The web portal is the face of the Zenoss system and is the place where we spend most of our time. It's an AJAX enabled interface that provides a single access point to the monitoring system and requires no operating-system-specific knowledge to use. The web interface features drag-and-drop dashboard portlets that display a customized view of our network's health at any given time. The following screen capture shows the web portal.

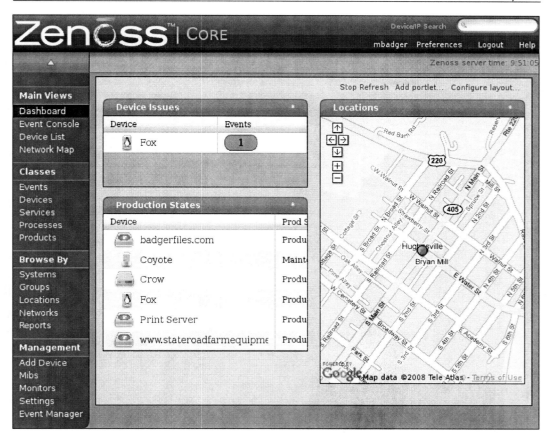

Device Management

At the heart of the device management, Zenoss places a configuration management database (CMDB), which stores a model of the IT environment and its change history. Zenoss supports adding devices to the CMDB one at a time or by auto-discovering active devices by walking the routing tables. Devices are then modeled via simple network management protocol (SNMP), SSH, or port scans.

Zenoss allows us to organize devices by user-defined locations, groups, and systems. One of the Zenoss's most powerful organizational concepts is classes, which allow us to define monitoring characteristics based on a hierarchical classification of devices. The following screen capture provides a look at a device status page.

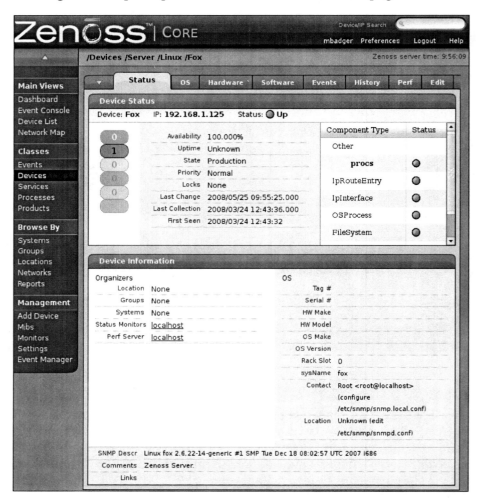

Availability and Performance Monitors

By using ICMP and SNMP monitoring, Zenoss reports on the availability of the following:

- Network devices
- TCP/IP services and ports

- URL availability
- Windows services and processes
- Linux/UNIX processes

Zenoss monitors are Level-3 network topology aware, which reduces the amount of alert chatter by creating an event about the problem device only and not about the devices that depend on the down device.

Zenoss Core 2.1 introduces a Flash-based map of the network topology that displays a view of the network on a single page, which can be seen in the following screen capture.

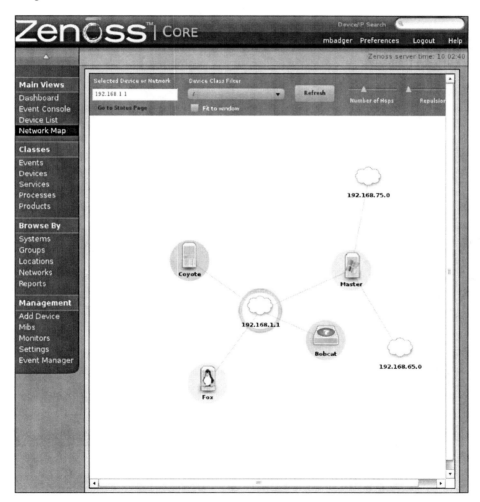

Zenoss integrates Google Maps to provide a high level geographic status of the user-defined network locations at the city, state/province, or country level. The following screen capture shows a view of the Google Maps integration.

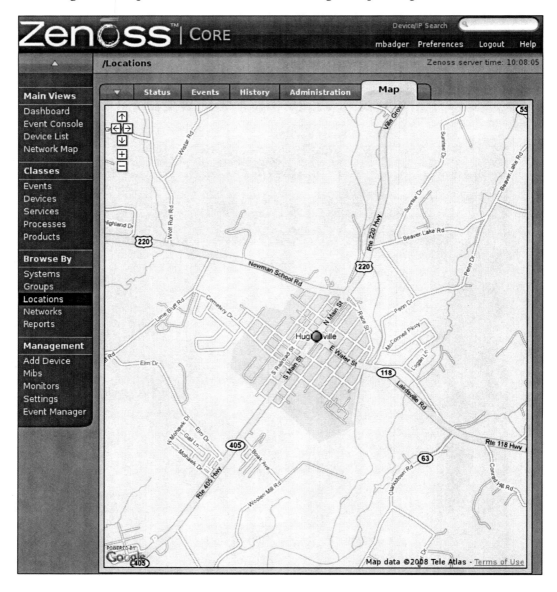

Performance monitors collect time series data and provide us with a graphical analysis of the following components:

- File system statistics
- CPU and memory usage
- JMX monitoring for J2EE servers
- Nagios and Cacti plug-in support

If a monitored device crosses a defined threshold, Zenoss generates an event.

Event Management

Zenoss monitors a variety of sources for signs of trouble, including syslogs, availability and performance monitors, SNMP traps, and Windows event logs. Core features of the event management system include:

- Custom events
- Automatic prioritization
- Event deduplication
- Up/down event correlation

Zenoss processes events based on a customizable set of rules. In response to events, Zenoss can send email or pager alerts, run a script, or do nothing. We can configure how Zenoss responds to an event by defining alerting rules for users and groups.

System Reports

Zenoss packages a set of standard reports that allow us to view what is happening right now, as well as what has happened. The reports integrate with the device management, performance monitors, events and user functionalities of Zenoss. Advanced users can create custom reports as needed.

Zenoss Inc.

Zenoss Core is backed by the commercial company, Zenoss Inc., which was co-founded by Erik Dahl and Bill Karpovich in 2006. Prior to founding Zenoss Inc., Dahl began development of Zenoss in 2002 to address a need he saw in the enterprise-systems monitoring market. He did this by setting out to develop an affordable, functional, and easy to use solution for organizations of all sizes.

In addition to sponsoring the development of Zenoss Core, Zenoss Inc. provides consulting, training, paid support, and an enterprise edition of Zenoss. Zenoss Enterprise extends the functionality of Zenoss Core by offering an extended report library, synthetic web transactions, certified monitors (ZenPacks), and a global dashboard for multiple Zenoss installations.

Today, Zenoss Inc. makes systems and network monitoring available to everyone under the GPL v2 license.

Summary

Now that we have an overview of Zenoss Core's network and systems management capabilities, we will examine the technical structure. Chapter 2 discusses the system architecture of Zenoss Core and introduces the major components that make the application work.

2
System Architecture

Zenoss blends innovative development with several open-source software projects to create a robust network and systems management solution. Before we jump into installation, we can pause for a moment to take a peek under the hood and see what makes Zenoss work. Reviewing the system architecture now provides us with an understanding that can help troubleshoot problems that may arise later.

Zenoss provides everything that we need to discover, collect, store, and manage our IT resources; and when we talk about the system architecture, it helps to conceptually segregate Zenoss into three layers:

- User
- Data
- Collection

The **User Layer** (refer to the following screenshot) allows us to connect to the Zenoss from any computer running Mozilla Firefox or Microsoft Internet Explorer. From the **User Layer**, we manage the device data that Zenoss collects from our network. Although Zenoss automatically handles many collection and monitoring tasks, we can manually control the collection components from the Zenoss web interface.

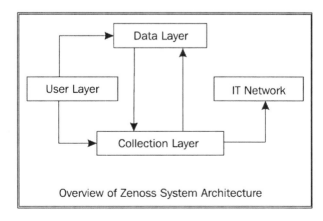

Overview of Zenoss System Architecture

The most notable open-source software components that integrate with Zenoss include Zope, Python, MySQL, RRDtool, and Twisted. In this Chapter, we will examine each layer and its core components.

User Layer

Zenoss is flexible enough to work from a command line, but most of our work will take place via an AJAX enabled interface, which is based on the Zope application server framework. We limit our command line work to installation, troubleshooting, and general curiosity.

The following screenshot shows the view of the Zenoss dashboard.

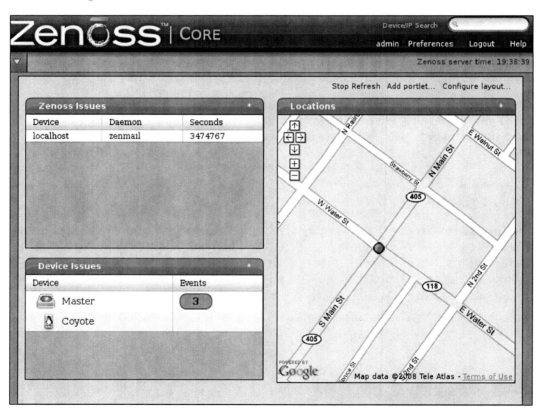

Zope is a popular, extensible application server written in Python. It features a built-in web server, transactional object database, and HTML templates. Python has a reputation as an easy-to-use object-oriented programming language. Not only is Python the basis for Zope, it's also the basis for Zenoss Core.

Through the web interface, we provide input with both the data and collection layers to accomplish tasks related to the following areas:

- Navigation and organization
- Device management
- Availability and performance monitors
- System reports
- Event Management
- Settings and Administration

Data Layer

As we might expect, databases are the heart of the data layer, and Zenoss stores data in three types of databases. The **Collection** layer funnels device information to **ZenHub**, which in turns stores the data in the appropriate place. (Refer to the following screenshot).

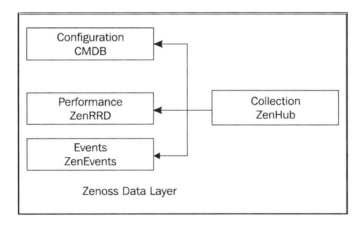

Events are stored in a MySQL database. Zenoss generates **Events** when an established threshold is crossed, such as a server outage or high memory usage. **Events** trigger actions, such as email or pager alerts.

MySQL is a popular open-source database commonly used by web applications as part of the LAMP (Linux, Apache, MySQL, and PHP) stack. It is often praised in the industry for being fast and reliable.

Time series performance gets stored in a Round Robin Database (RRD). A round robin database differs from a linear database, such as MySQL, in that it's circular — which means the size does not increase over time. Data is stored in a first in, first out basis. RRDtool provides Zenoss with the ability to log and graph performance data.

The third database deployed by Zenoss is a Configuration Management Database (**CMDB**). The **CMDB** is an Information Technology Infrastructure Library (ITIL) standard for managing the configuration, relationship, and change history of the IT environment, which creates a detailed model of the network. Zenoss uses a Zope object database to house the **CMDB**.

Collection Layer

The collection layer includes several daemons that gather information about devices, performance, and **Events** (refer to the following screen capture). They feed information to **ZenHub** to distribute to the appropriate database. As we'll find out, the Zenoss daemons are easy to identify — they all start with the prefix "zen."

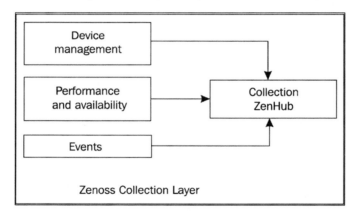

We access the daemons by selecting **Settings > Daemons** from the Zenoss dashboard. As the following screen capture illustrates, the dashboard provides us with the complete view of the **Zenoss Daemons** that includes the process ID and up/down **State**. Green is up; red is down. Also from the interface, we can view the log, edit the **Configuration**, and start and **Stop** each daemon.

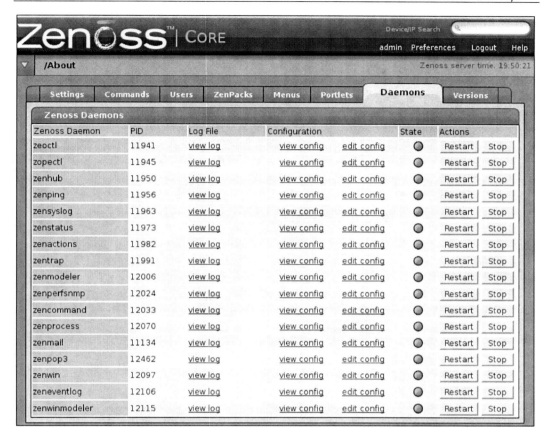

If we browse the file system, we will find each daemon in $ZENHOME/bin. $ZENHOME is an environment variable, which allows us to talk about the Zenoss installation directory without knowing exactly where it is. For example, I may install to /usr/local/zenoss while you install to /home/zenoss.

Twisted is an integral network communication protocol for the daemons. The Twisted Core README file describes Twisted as an "event based framework for internet applications, which works on Python 2.3.x or 2.4.x"

Device Management

Finding the devices on our networks is a prerequisite to managing them, and Zenoss not only finds the devices, it models them. Device modeling builds a detailed overview of the network by recording the following types of information: system dependencies, available services, and change history.

Zenoss provides several ways to view information about a device or a group of devices. The following screen capture shows an alphabetical list of all devices from the **Device List** view.

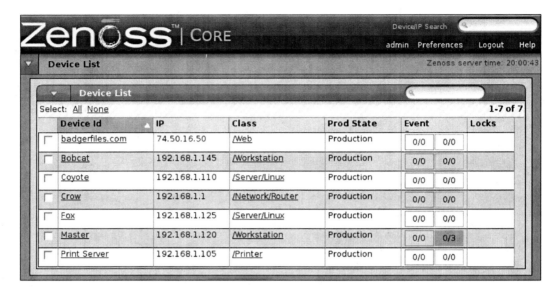

The following table describes the daemons responsible for discovering and modeling devices.

Device Daemon	Description
zenmodeler	Queries the devices via SSH, SNMP, and port scans when we model the device. Each time zenmodeler runs on a device, it compares its findings with existing configuration and updates it as necessary.
zendisc	Runs when we add a network subnet to Zenoss and choose to discover all devices attached to the network.

Zenoss uses Simple Network Management Protocol (SNMP) as a primary collection protocol.

Performance And Availability

The Zenoss performance and availability daemons help us determine if the devices on our network are available and performing within the established guidelines. If our monitored systems perform in an unexpected way, Zenoss generates an event. The following screen capture displays an overview of the **Device Status** for a server.

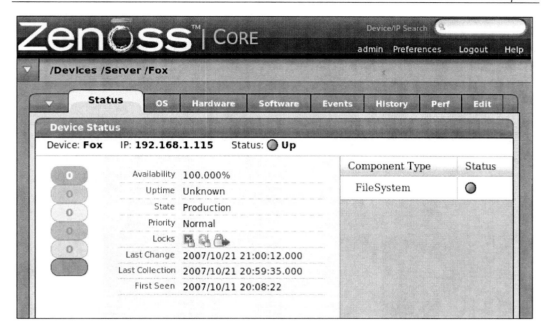

The following daemons play an important role in collecting performance and availability data.

Performance Daemon	Description
zenperfsnmp	Stores the collected performance data in RRD files so that RRDtool can graph device performance over hourly, daily, weekly, monthly, or yearly durations.
zencommand	Provides a way to run custom scripts and third party plug-ins including Nagios and Cacti plug-ins from within Zenoss.
zenprocess	Monitors performance data, such as CPU and Memory usage using SNMP collection.
zenping	Pings a device and reports an up or down status. This is the main way Zenoss knows if the device is active or not. Zenping is layer-3 topology aware, which means that if a router goes down, Zenoss will know the devices dependent on the router are also unreachable and will not monitor them during the outage.
zenstatus	Tests the TCP ports and reports an up or down service.

Event Information

When a device goes down or a service crosses a predetermined threshold, such as available disk space, Zenoss generates an event. One of the ways Zenoss displays monitoring activity is via the **Event Console**, as shown in the following screen capture.

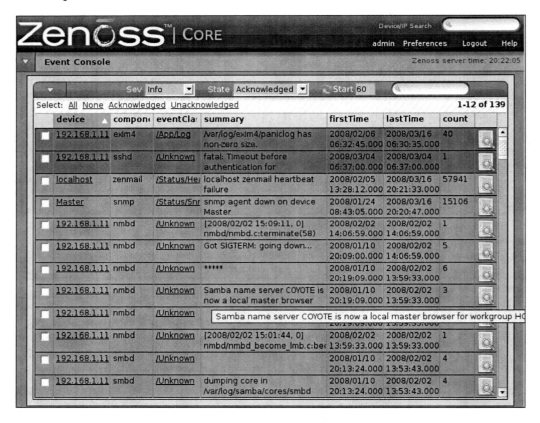

We can configure Zenoss to notify us by email or pager when events occur. Zenoss can also automatically run custom commands in response to events as a first step in problem resolution.

Event Daemon	Description
zensyslog	Creates events from syslog messages.
zeneventlog	Creates events from Windows event logs.
zentrap	Creates events from SNMP traps. When a problem occurs on a monitored device, it generates an SNMP trap to alert Zenoss of the problem.

Summary

At a high level, we want to find and monitor devices, then be notified when problems occur. The Zenoss web interface lets us do that without thinking too much about the internal components. By reviewing the system architecture, we gained a cursory understanding about how Zenoss works, which provided a foundation for configuration, troubleshooting, and advanced usage. We did not cover all of the Zenoss commands or open-source components, but we did highlight the aspects of the system we will work with, throughout the book. Now, we're ready to install a working Zenoss system. Chapter 3 identifies the Zenoss dependencies, walks through each of the installation options, and prepares our network servers for monitoring.

3
Installation and Set up

In this chapter, we fill in the step-by-step details required to get a functioning Zenoss system. We identify dependencies, review installation options, and take a look at server setup.

Our first step is to choose one of the three installation methods: virtual appliance, binary installer, or source. The virtual appliance makes a good choice, if we want to evaluate or demonstrate Zenoss. The virtual appliance runs a functional Zenoss system using VMware Player or VMware Server out-of-the-box and needs no Linux knowledge. When run from VMware, the Zenoss virtual appliance may be used to monitor networks with relatively few devices.

The binary installer makes a good choice if we want to avoid building Zenoss from source and we run a supported distribution. The Supported Operating Systems section in this chapter includes a list of distributions that have binary installation support.

We can build from source on a variety of Unix-based environments, such as Ubuntu and Mac OS X. A source installation gives us the ability to install Zenoss in the environment of our choice but requires more work. Of the three installation methods, a source install requires the most familiarity with your operating system and presents more points of failure.

As we move beyond installing Zenoss to set up, we focus on firewall policies and Simple Network Management Protocol (SNMP) for Linux and Windows systems. Even though Zenoss can use other methods to monitor devices, SNMP is the default monitoring protocol. We are free to change how we monitor and collect information at any time.

During the installation and the set up, we work from the command line because it's fast and it's consistent from one distribution to the next. If an error does occur, we can see the error immediately printed to the terminal window.

When working from the command line, we assume knowledge of two basic tasks: opening the terminal window and navigating the file structure. For all other tasks, the book provides the exact command to type.

After installation and set up, we spend most of our time working with Zenoss through the web interface. Let's get this installation out of the way so we can discover Zenoss.

Server Specifications

Actual server specifications may vary depending on the amount and frequency of the data you collect. Zenoss Inc. recommends the following hardware specifications as a starting point based on feedback from the community:

- Network with up to 250 devices
  - ° 4 GB RAM
  - ° Core 2 Duo E6300 1.86/1066 RTL
  - ° 75 GB disk storage
- Network with more than 250 devices

  - ° 8 GB RAM
  - ° XEON 5120 DC 1.86/1066/4MB
  - ° Four 75 GB drives in two RAID-1 pairs

Supported Operating Systems

Zenoss requires a Unix-based platform and installs on systems capable of running a GNU build environment. However, Zenoss supports only a few distributions with binary installers. The following table shows the available installation options.

Installation Type	Platform
Virtual Appliance	Windows Linux
Binary Installer	Red Hat Enterprise Linux 5 Fedora Core 6 SUSE
Source	Ubuntu FreeBSD Solaris 10 Mac OS X Other Linux environments

As more binary installers become available, Zenoss posts them to
http://www.zenoss.com/download.

Zenoss Dependencies

Virtual appliance users do not need to install any dependencies because they are
included in the image. For all other installations, you need to install the following
software packages prior to installing Zenoss:

- MySQL 5.0.22 or higher
- MySQL development environment
- Python 2.3.5 or 2.4
- Python development environment

If you plan to build a Zenoss installation from source code, you need to install
the following:

- SWIG
- Autoconf
- GNU build environment

Dependent software packages are available via your distribution's normal software
package manager. However, the package names and installation commands
vary based on distribution. Consult your distribution's documentation for
more information.

Quick Start with Virtual Appliance

If we know how to download and install software in our host environment, we
can get a working Zenoss system with the virtual appliance. The Zenoss virtual
appliance packages a working Zenoss Core installation inside a Linux guest that can
be booted from a host system, including Windows, using VMware's Player, Server,
or Workstation programs.

The virtual appliance is great for:

- Users with little or no Linux knowledge
- Demonstrations and Evaluations
- Monitoring small networks with a few devices

Install Virtual Appliance

We will finish the installation as fast as we can download files and install the VMware Player. Let's begin:

1. Download the VMware Player from `http://www.vmware.com/player/`. Registration is required to complete the download.

2. Install VMware Player according to VMware's installation instructions for your operating system.

3. Download the Zenoss virtual appliance from `http://www.zenoss.com/download/`.

4. Unzip the Zenoss virtual appliance download file to a working directory in your system.

5. Open **VMware Player**:
   - On Windows, select **Start > Programs > VMware Player**.
   - On Linux, select VMplayer from the application menu, or type the command:

     `vmware`

6. **VMware Player** prompts us to load the virtual machine configuration file we previously unzipped, as shown in the following screenshot:

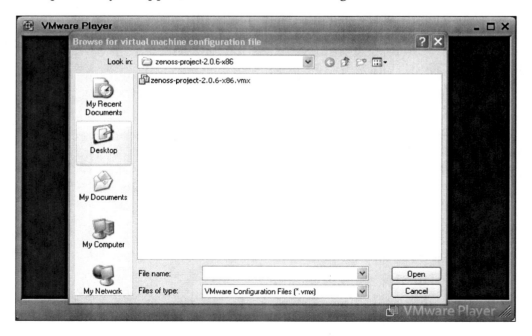

7. Open the Zenoss virtual appliance we unzipped in step 4.

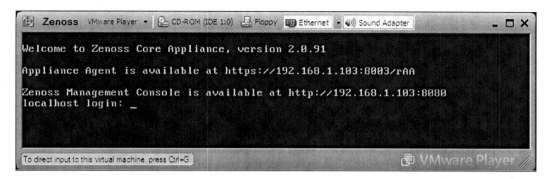

The Zenoss virtual appliance takes a few minutes to load depending on the performance of your system. When the appliance boots, a welcome window opens and displays the IP address of the Zenoss management console and the standard Linux login prompt, as shown in the following screenshot:

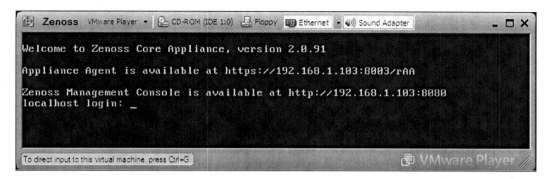

When we connect to Zenoss through our web browser, we use the IP address of the Zenoss management console that displays on the welcome screen (e.g. http://192.168.1.125.8080). We cannot access our virtualized Zenoss installation by navigating to localhost, which is the host name of the Zenoss virtual appliance. If the IP address of the Zenoss console does not display, we can obtain the IP address using the ifconfig command, as described in the next section: Working with The Virtual Appliance.

Zenoss is ready to monitor. Our next step is to set up the servers on our network to be monitored. If you can't wait to see Zenoss in action, feel free to skip the server setup section for now and check out Chapter 4 for an introduction to web interface. You can come back and set up your servers later.

If this is the first time you are working with VMware or Linux, take a few minutes to get acquainted with the environment.

Working with The Virtual Appliance

The Zenoss virtual appliance is a streamlined but functional Linux system, which means we can log in and have access to the underlying Linux environment. Let's cover a few basic tasks.

In order to type inside the virtual appliance window, use the keyboard shortcut:

Ctrl + G

To return the cursor to the host desktop, use the keyboard shortcut:

Ctrl + Alt

By default, the root login does not have a password assigned. To log in to the virtual appliance, enter the following user name at the login prompt:

`root`

To set a password for the root user, enter the command:

`passwd`

The passwd command prompts us to enter a new password. Assigning a password to the root user makes the system more secure and allows us to connect to the virtual appliance as root via SSH.

The IP address of the Zenoss virtual appliance is displayed at the top of the terminal window when the appliance loads. The most confusing part about using the Zenoss virtual appliance may be picking the correct IP address and port number. We connect to Zenoss on port 8080. So if our virtual appliance has an IP address of 192.168.1.103, then we use `http://192.168.1.103:8080` to open the Zenoss login screen. If we use port 8003, we access the rPath management console, which is the underlying system used to build the Zenoss virtual appliance.

After login, we can find additional IP configuration as shown in the following screenshot, with the command:

`ifconfig`

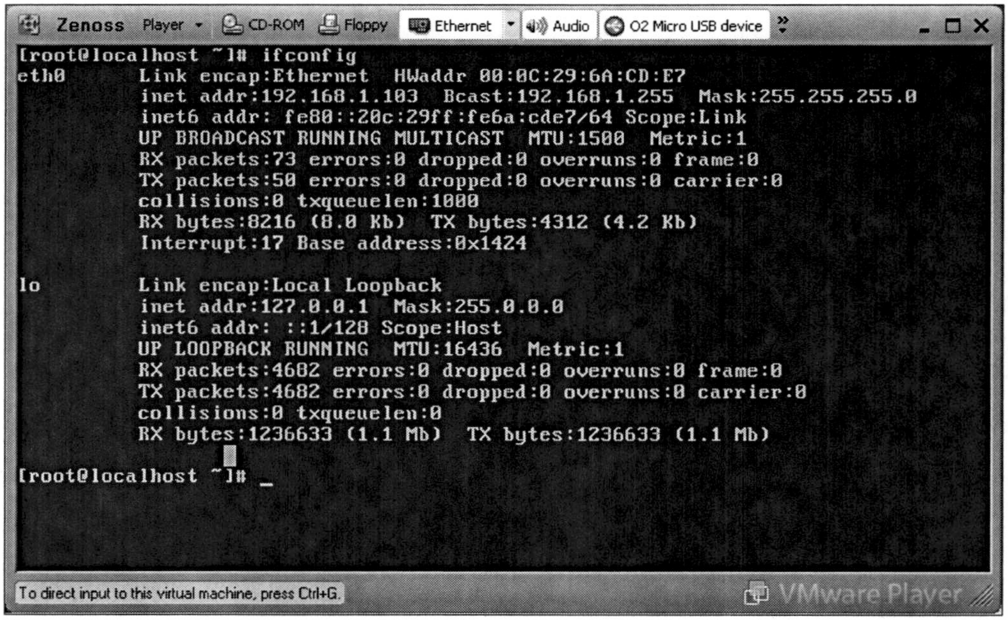

To shut down the virtual appliance, select **Player > Exit** from the VMware Player. We may also use the the command:

```
shutdown -h now
```

If we shut down the virtual appliance, Zenoss no longer monitors the network and the web interface is not accessible.

We may now jump ahead to the Server Setup section of this chapter for help in configuring the servers we wish to monitor.

Binary Installation

Zenoss provides a binary installer in RPM format for Red Hat Enterprise Linux, which covers CentOS and Fedora Core. Binaries for additional distributions are added by Zenoss as the market demands and as time allows.

To install Zenoss and its dependencies on Red Hat:

1. Download the latest RPM for Red Hat Enterprise Linux from http://www.zenoss.com/download/.

2. Open a terminal window and become the root user:
   ```
   su -
   ```

3. If you have not yet installed the Zenoss dependencies, run:
   ```
   yum -y install mysql mysql-server net-snmp net-snmp-utils /
   python python-dev
   ```

4. Install the Zenoss RPM by running the following command from the download directory where x.x-x equals the latest version number:
   ```
   rpm -ivh zenoss-2.x.x-x.el5.i386.rpm
   ```

5. Start SNMP:
   ```
   service snmp start
   ```

6. Start MySQL:
   ```
   service mysqld start
   ```

7. Start Zenoss:
   ```
   /etc/init.d/zenoss start
   ```

Let's test our installation. Open a browser and enter the URL of the Zenoss server, which listens on port 8080 (for example `http://192.168.115:8080`). A screen appears as shown in the following screenshot.

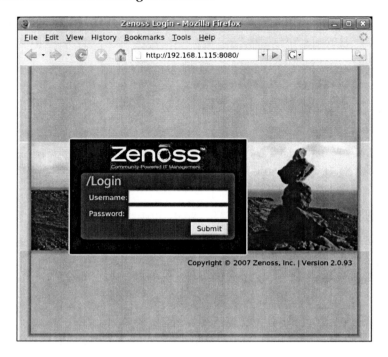

Chapter 4 tells us more about logging in and using the web interface. For more setup information, continue with the Server Setup section.

Source Installation

Like any open-source project, we can install Zenoss using the source code on any Linux- or Unix-based system including FreeBSD, Mac OS X, and Ubuntu. The installation requires more setup, but in return for the extra work, we are able to extend Zenoss to a variety of architectures.

Distribution-specific tips for Ubuntu users are included in the Ubuntu Notes section to help make the installation smoother. Additional distribution notes can be found in the `INSTALL.TXT` file located in the top level of the source code directory.

Ubuntu Notes

The Ubuntu installation generally follows the same installation steps as the source install, but the following information will help us get started.

Debian derivative distributions use APT to add, update, and remove software packages from the system. We can use APT from the command line or from the graphical interface Synaptic, available from the **System > Administration** menu in Ubuntu. Update the repositories with the following two commands:

```
sudo apt-get update
sudo apt-get upgrade
```

Now, install the Zenoss dependencies with apt-get. The example commands specify each package installation command on a separate line for clarity.

```
sudo apt-get install mysql-server
sudo apt-get install mysql-client
sudo apt-get install libmysqlclient15-dev
sudo apt-get install python2.4
sudo apt-get install python2.4-dev
sudo apt-get install build-essential
sudo apt-get install snmp
sudo apt-get install snmpd
sudo apt-get install autoconf
sudo apt-get install swig
sudo apt-get install python-setuptools
```

To reduce the amount of typing, we may supply all the package names as arguments to the apt-get install command. For example:

```
sudo apt-get install mysql-server mysql-client ...
```

Ubuntu installs Python 2.5, but Zenoss requires we install Python 2.4 to properly build all of its dependencies. Prior to starting the Zenoss installation, update the /usr/bin/python symlink to point to the python2.4 file:

```
unlink /usr/bin/python
ln -s /usr/bin/python2.4 /usr/bin/python
```

After the installation, you can change the /usr/bin/python symlink back as follows:

```
unlink /usr/bin/python
ln -s /usr/bin/pythong2.5 /usr/bin/python
```

From this point, follow the source installation procedures to set up and install Zenoss.

System Setup for Source Install

Open a terminal window and become the root user:

1. Install the dependencies listed earlier in this chapter.

2. Create the Zenoss user:

    ```
    useradd zenoss
    ```

3. Add the ZENHOME and PYTHONPATH environment variables to the zenoss user's environment by adding the following lines to the zenoss user's .bashrc file (as shown in the following screenshot):

    ◦   export ZENHOME=/usr/local/zenoss

    ◦   export PYTHONPATH=$ZENHOME/lib/python

    ◦   export PATH=$ZENHOME/bin:$PATH

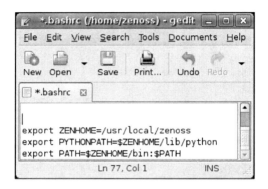

4. Create the installation directory:

    ```
    mkdir /usr/local/zenoss
    ```

5. Change the installation directory's ownership to the zenoss user:

    ```
    chown zenoss /usr/local/zenoss
    ```

We can install Zenoss to any directory, but we must set the ZENHOME environment variable in the .bashrc file to match the installation directory.

Download Zenoss Source

Next, we download the Zenoss source file from http://www.zenoss.com/download and unpack it to a working directory on the Zenoss server with the following command, where x.x-x equals the latest version:

```
tar xzvf zenoss-2.x.x-x.tar.gz
```

When we build and install Zenoss, we work as the user zenoss, which presents some permission problems during the build, if we download the files as a user other than zenoss. As root, use the following commands to move the source files to /home/zenoss and set ownership:

```
mv zenoss-2.x.x-x /home/zenoss
chown -R zenoss /home/zenoss/zenoss-2.x.x-x
```

We are ready to build the source code.

Build And Install Zenoss

To build and install Zenoss, we run the included `install.sh` script. The script collects configuration information for the web and database components of the Zenoss system, then builds the source files.

We continue our work from the command line:

1. Log in as the user zenoss:

   `su - zenoss`

2. From the Zenoss source directory, run the install script:

   `./install.sh`

3. The install script prompts for the following Zenoss database configurations (refer to the following screenshot):

   ° Admin password for the dashboard
   ° The host name of the MySQL server
   ° A root user for the MySQL server
   ° A password for the MySQL root user
   ° Name of the MySQL events database
   ° A user name for the events database
   ° Password for the events database user name

```
zenoss@coyote: /home/mike/Desktop/zenoss-2.0.91

File  Edit  View  Terminal  Tabs  Help
zenoss@coyote:/home/mike/Desktop/zenoss-2.0.91$ ./install.sh

This installer actually builds Zenoss.
For a simpler installation try the VMPlayer Appliance image,
or use RPMs for Redhat based systems.

Building...

Password for the Zenoss "admin" user [zenoss]:
Enter the password again:
/usr/local/zenoss already exists!
Stopping zenoss
Do you want me to keep your existing database? (Y/n) n

MySQL server hostname [localhost]:
MySQL server root username [root]:
MySQL server root password []:
MySQL event database name [events]:
MySQL username for Zenoss events database [zenoss]:
MySQL password for zenoss [zenoss]:
installing into //usr/local/zenoss
build log is in zenbuild.log
unpacking Zope-2.8.8-final in build/
configuring build/Zope-2.8.8-final/makefile
installing libzenos/Products.tar.gz
installing libzenos/bin.tar.gz
installing libzenos/extras.tar.gz
mkdir -p //usr/local/zenoss/skel/etc
cp conf/zope.conf.in //usr/local/zenoss/skel/etc/zenoss.conf.in
installing zope
```

4. After the install completes, set ownership and uid on zensocket. As root, enter the following commands:

```
chown root:zenoss /usr/local/zenoss/bin/zensocket
chmod 04750 /usr/local/zenoss/bin/zensocket
```

If the installation fails, the error message prints to the terminal window and to the zenbuild.log file in the installation source directory. Source installations most often fail because the dependencies are not properly installed.

To continue with a failed installation after we fix the problem, clean the installation source, and run the install script again with the commands:

```
make clean
./install.sh
```

The "make clean" command removes the build files and zenbuild.log file.

After a successful installation, we can log in to Zenoss by navigating to port 8080 of the Zenoss server (e.g., http://192.168.1.115:8080)

Server Setup

The second part of the installation equation is server setup. We'll examine the following configuration options:

- Start Zenoss at boot time
- Firewall policies
- SNMP on Linux and Windows

Start Zenoss at Boot Time

By default, Zenoss does not automatically start during the boot process and it is required to start the Zenoss daemons manually. As the zenoss user, run the command:

```
zenoss start
```

Red Hat users can enable Zenoss at boot time by running the following commands as root:

```
/sbin/chkconfig zenoss
/sbin/chkconfig --level 345 zenoss on
```

If you use a Debian based distribution, such as Ubuntu, do the following as root:

```
cp /usr/local/zenoss/bin/zenoss /etc/init.d/
update-rc.d zenoss defaults 95
```

The next time the system reboots, use the following command as the zenoss user to verify whether Zenoss started:

```
zenoss status
```

If the Zenoss daemons are not running, consult your distribution's documentation for help in automatically starting programs at boot time. Remember, we can run the following command as the zenoss user to start Zenoss:

```
zenoss start
```

Firewall Policies

Zenoss requires access to a few ports on the network in order to communicate with the the systems we want to monitor. The Zenoss server needs to accept connections on the following ports:

- 8080 for HTTP access
- 514 for syslog access
- 22 for SSH access

To facilitate monitoring, the systems on the network need to allow access to the following ports:

- 161 for SNMP
- 22 for SSH

This is a common list of ports, but network and monitoring needs are unique from one site to the next. For example, if you do not plan to connect to your Zenoss server via SSH, then you do not need to open port 22.

Iptables is a popular tool for managing firewall access on Linux systems. Firestarter, a graphical front end to iptables is shown in the following screenshot. Windows has built-in firewall support via the Windows Firewall Control Panel (as shown in the screenshot following the next one). If you are unsure about how to configure port access, consult your firewall documentation or system administrator.

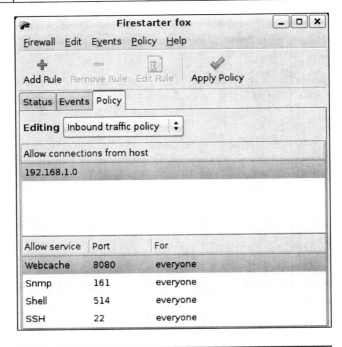

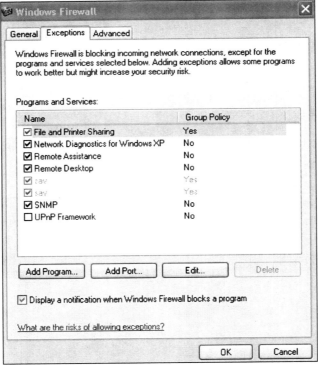

SNMP on Linux

Zenoss uses SNMP to collect information, such as file system statistics, memory usage, and interface status from the systems attached to the network. The network devices report data to Zenoss via an SNMP agent, which is installed on each device, but SNMP is only a collection protocol. The information SNMP collects about each device depends on the device's Management Information base (MIB). MIBs are management, that define the devices on the network and are part of the OSI network management model. MIBs further rely on object identifiers (OIDs) to tell SNMP which data values to return.

As we will see in later chapters, Zenoss can discover and monitor our networks without using SNMP, but if we choose not to use SNMP, we sacrifice a detailed model of our networks.

Install SNMP on Linux

If we plan to collect device information from the network using SNMP, we need to install SNMP on the Zenoss server and the devices attached to the network. The package names vary from one distribution to the next, so be sure to check with your distribution, if you are unsure of which file you need.

Red Hat users can install SNMP with the command:

```
yum -y install net-snmp
```

Ubuntu users can install SNMP with the command:

```
apt-get install snmpd
```

Zenoss recommends we add several configuration changes to the snmpd.conf file. Before you make any changes, back up the snmpd.conf file. As root:

```
cp /etc/snmp/snmpd.conf /etc/snmp/snmpd.conf.bak
```

In the section that begins "First, map the community name into a security name," add:

```
    com2sec notConfigUser default public
```

In the section that begins "Second, map the security names into group names," add:

```
    group notConfigGroup v1 notConfigUser
    group notConfigGroup v2c notConfigUser
```

In the section that begins "Third, create a view for us to let the groups have rights," add:

```
view systemview included .1
```

In the section that begins, "Finally, grant the 2 groups access to the 1 view with different write permissions," add the following line:

```
access notConfigGroup  ""     any    noauth exact systemview    none
none
```

Add the following lines to the System Contact Information section:

```
syslocation Unknown (edit /etc/snmp/snmpd.local.conf)
syscontact Root <root@localhost> (configure /etc/snmp/snmpd.local.
conf)
```

Add the following lines to the Further Information section to configure the default community string for sending traps:

```
trapcommunity public
trapsink default
```

WMI And SNMP on Windows

Often, we want to know more about our Windows servers than a simple up or down status. In order to view specific information about Windows services and events, we need to enable Windows Management Instrumentation (WMI) and SNMP.

WMI provides several management options for Windows 2000, Windows XP, and Windows Server 2003, including the ability to access Windows event logs.

WMI and SNMP are enabled from the Windows Management and Monitoring Tools packages. To install WMI and SNMP (refer to the following screenshot):

1. Open the Windows Control Panel.
2. Select Add/Remove **Windows Components**.
3. Click on **Management and Monitoring Tools** and select **Details**.
4. Select **Simple Network Management Protocol** and **WMI**.

5. Save the changes to install the **Windows Components**.

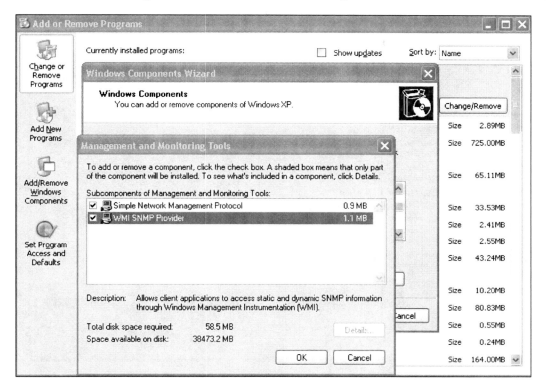

After WMI installs, we can get detailed information about the services running on server and confirm WMI is properly configured. From the Windows Computer Management control panel:

1. Run the command wbemtest from Start > Run.
2. Select the Connect. button.
3. Change the Namespace field to \\HOST\root\cimv2.
4. Enter user name and password.

5. Click the Query button.

6. In the search box, type "**select * from win32_service**" to see a list of services as shown in the next screen capture.

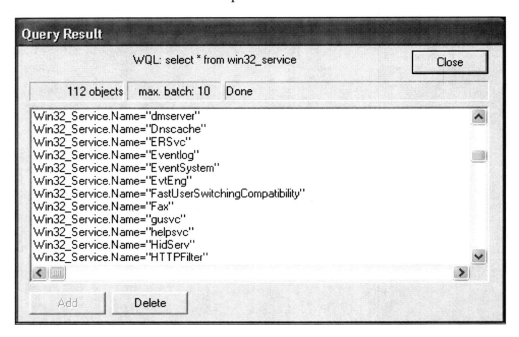

The Windows SNMP agent does not return information about the server's CPU, memory, or file system. For these stats, Zenoss Inc. recommends we install the third-party SNMP Informant from `http://www.snmp-informant.com`. No configuration is necessary for SNMP Informant.

Summary

In this chapter we examined the Zenoss installation from several angles, and we found an installation type that meets our abilities and needs. We prepared the servers on our network for monitoring by configuring SNMP and we opened the necessary firewall access to our systems.

Now that we have a functioning Zenoss system, we turn to Chapter 4 for our first look at the Zenoss web interface, the heart of the system. We take an in-depth tour of Zenoss' navigation, organization, and setup features, and we begin to configure our monitoring environment.

The Zenoss User Interface

4

Before we jump straight into monitoring and modeling devices, we need to cover a few concepts that will help us manage our device data. If we have not yet thought about our device hierarchies, we will raise those questions as we move through the chapter. Our device hierarchies establish relationships to with other devices, locations, systems, and groups.

In this chapter, we log in and explore the interface using four types of navigation techniques: navigation panel, bread crumbs, page tabs, and table menus. As we navigate the Zenoss interface, we create organizers to help us build device relationships.

Establishing device relationships help us understand how a device fits into our IT environment by location, system, group, and class. The relationships we build in this chapter help us manage our devices by assigning common configurations to a group of devices. The groupings provide all devices a way to inherit the configurations of a common organizer.

To demonstrate Zenoss' hierarchy and inheritance concepts, we need devices to organize, so we'll let Zenoss auto-discover the devices on our networks. The auto-discovery process provides a quick way to build an inventory of the devices on the network and jump-start our monitoring process.

Welcome to Zenoss

Open a web browser and go to `http://zenoss-server:8080`, where `zenoss-server` is the URL of the machine you installed Zenoss on. Notice the port number? Zenoss listens on port 8080.

When prompted for a user name and password, enter the values you defined during setup. The defaults are:

- **User name: admin**
- **Password: zenoss**

The following screenshot shows the Zenoss login screen.

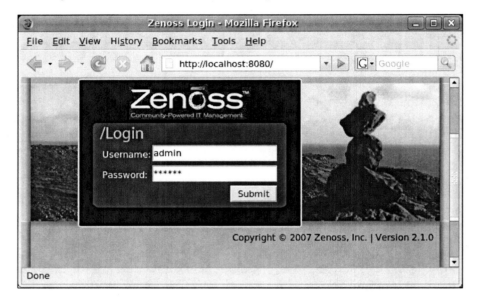

After a successful login, the Zenoss interface displays the default dashboard view, which includes drag-and-drop portlets for Locations, Device Issues, and Zenoss Issues. Additional portlets are available from the Add Portlets link.

Navigation Techniques

At first look, the interface to the Zenoss web application appears overwhelming and we don't have any big red buttons that say, "start here." As we take a few minutes to acquaint ourselves with the application, the overwhelming feeling will subside.

The navigation panel runs down the left side of the screen and contains headings for **Main Views, Classes, Browse By**, and **Management**. The navigation panel provides the primary way to move from one section to the next within Zenoss (refer to the following screen capture).

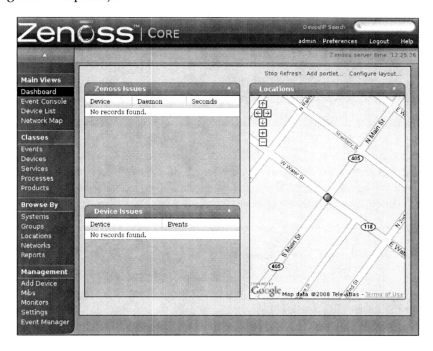

To hide the navigation panel, click the triangle located above the **Main Views** heading. When the panel is hidden, the triangle inverts and the screen automatically resizes to give the page content more space. Click on the inverted triangle to display the panel, and pin the panel in place by clicking the tack.

While the navigation panel allows us to quickly navigate the system, Zenoss uses bread crumb links to help us know where we have been and where we are in the application. If you have used other web applications, such as wikis, you must be familiar with breadcrumb navigation.

To see the bread crumbs in action, select **Devices** from the navigation panel. Click on **Server** from the list of sub-devices, then Linux. The bread crumbs display a navigable path which can be found directly under the Zenoss Core log, and based on our example, we see **/Devices/Server/Linux** (as shown in the following screenshot). Each time we select a sub-device or device, the bread crumbs update to reflect the current location. To get back to the list of Server sub-devices, click on the **Server** link in the bread crumbs.

From **/Devices/Server**, we notice a third navigation method, tabs. Tabs should be fairly self explanatory in that we click on the tab and a new screen displays. Zenoss uses the tabs to display information and configurations specific to the device you are on. The following screenshot shows the view of tabs within a page.

The fourth level of navigation occurs on the tables that display on each page. The inverted white triangles next to **Classes**, **Sub-Devices**, and **Devices** represent the table menus and display context sensitive options. Most of what we do to manipulate our monitoring environment will be based on the page menus. The following screenshot shows a sample table menu.

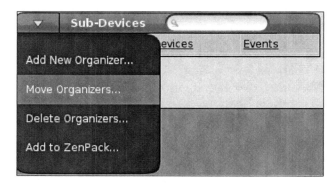

With an overview of the navigation techniques in place, we're ready to continue setting up our Zenoss system.

User Accounts

Zenoss is a multi-user system, so we should create a user account for ourselves and any other person who may use Zenoss. To add a user account:

1. Select Settings from the navigation panel.

2. Click on the Users tab.

3. From the User table menu, select Add New User.

4. Enter a user name and click OK.

5. Click on the new user name do display the user properties and make the following changes:

   • Enter a password.

   • Set the role to ZenManager.

6. Click Save.

Chapter 9 provides a step-by-step guide to adding and managing users, including a discussion about the roles. The ZenManager role gives us sufficient access permissions to add, edit, or delete our device inventory within Zenoss.

We may now click the Logout link at the top of the Zenoss interface and log in using our user account.

Main Views

The Zenoss interface opens to the Dashboard view, which contains a list of configurable, drag-and-drop portlets. Portlets are widgets we remove and add from the dashboard that provide an overview of our monitoring status. We can choose from the following portlets:

• Location

• Device Issues

• Zenoss Issues

• Top Level Organizers

• Watch List

• Production States

The **Location**, **Device Issues**, and **Zenoss Issues** portlets display by default, but we can remove them by clicking on the asterisk at the top-right corner of the portlet to show a settings panel, as seen in the following screenshot. From the settings panel, choose the **Remove Portlet** link.

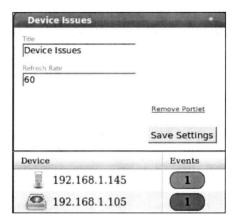

To add a portlet, click on the **Add Portlet** link at the top of the Dashboard view. From the **Add Portlet** dialog box that gets displayed, select the portlet you want to see on the Dashboard (refer to the following screenshot).

To arrange the portlets, click on the **Configure Layout** link at the top of the Dashboard view to display the **Column Layout** dialog box. We can choose from various combinations of one, two and three column arrangements. After we choose a layout, we can rearrange the order of the portlets on the screen by dragging and dropping a portlet to a new position on the screen.

Other main views include the Event Console, Device List, and Network Map. As we add devices and create events, we will talk about each of these in turn. For now, let's set up the Locations portlet to display **Google Maps**.

Locations with Google Maps

The Locations portlet not only displays our configured locations, but it also shows the network connections between our locations. The locations on the map also display the current status of the devices at a location and we can drill down to any device from the portlet.

In order to make the Locations portlet work, we need to add a Google Maps API key to the Zenoss settings. To acquire a Google Maps API key:

1. Visit `http://www.google.com/apis/google`.
2. Follow the "Sign up for a Google Maps API key" link.
3. Agree to the Google Maps license agreement .
4. Enter the URL of the Zenoss server to generate the key.
5. Copy the key.
6. Open Zenoss and click on Settings from the navigation panel.
7. Scroll to the bottom of the settings screen and paste the key into the field labeled Google Maps API Key.
8. Save the changes.

The page refreshes and displays a status message which says that we have successfully saved the settings. Navigate back to the Dashboard view by selecting Dashboard from the navigation panel. The Location portlet displays a map, but Google Maps doesn't know which specific location we want to see, so it guesses. We'll come back to locations in a while, but first, we need to finish our review of the Dashboard portlets.

Device Issues

The Device Issues portlet displays a list of all devices with an event using a color-coded status. Each device name is a hyperlink that links to the devices main status page. Likewise, clicking on the event redirects us to the event page for each device.

We can modify the portlet title and refresh rate from the settings pane.

Zenoss Issues

Zenoss not only monitors our network but it monitors itself and reports its status. If one of the daemons we discussed in Chapter 2 has a problem, Zenoss displays that problem in the **Zenoss Issues** portlet (refer to the following screenshot).

Like the Device Issues portlet, we can only change the portlet Title and Refresh Rate.

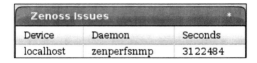

Watch List

With the **Watch List** portlet we can monitor the status of an entire device hierarchy, also known as a class, for example, **/Devices/Network**. If any device we classify as **Devices/Network** generates an event, the status updates on the **Watch List** portlet.

To watch a device class, select the class from the Zenoss Objects drop down menu that appears in the portlet settings. We can also change the **Title** and **Refresh Rate** (refer to the following screenshot).

Root Organizers

Zenoss allows us to organize our data in several ways, including by location, systems, groups, and devices. The **Root Organizers** portlet displays the status for the grouping we choose. The **Locations**, systems, and groups are user defined while the devices are primarily Zenoss defined.

The default organization is by device class. We configure locations, systems, and groups later in this chapter. If you want to select a new **Root Organizer**, choose the new organizer from the settings pane of the portlet. We can also change the portlet **Title** and **Refresh Rate** (refer to the following screenshot).

Production State

The **Production States** portlet displays the **Devices** assigned to the selected **Production State**. Default **Production States** are **Production, Pre-Production, Test, Maintenance,** and **Decommissioned**.

Select the **Production States** to display from the settings pane. To monitor multiple states, hold down the Ctrl key while selecting the states. You may also change the portlet **Title** and **Refresh Rate** (refer to the following screenshot).

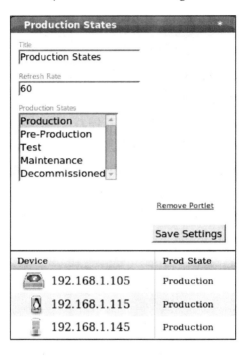

Browse By Organizers

We use the organizers in the Browse By category to define a classification hierarchy that lets us identify and manage our assets by systems, groups, locations, and networks. How we define our organizers depends on our monitoring environment and to what level we want to manage devices.

To demonstrate how we can organize our data, we'll create a sample company to monitor called Mill Race Communications. For the sake of our discussion, we'll assume the company has a support and development department with groups of staff in each department. We'll reference this sample company as we move through the Zenoss setup and the remainder of the book. We can change our organizers at any time.

We'll start by adding a location by selecting the **Locations** menu from the navigation panel (refer to the following screenshot).

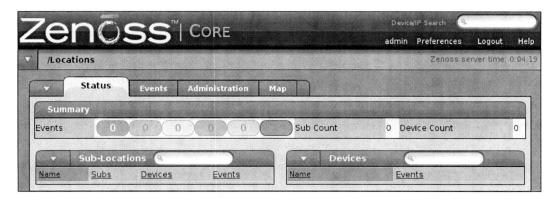

Locations

Location names can be generic or specific depending on individual needs. We use the locations to identify our network, so it's important to use values that have meaning. To enter a new location:

1. Select Add New Organizer from the Sub-Locations table menu.
2. Type a description (for example, Mill Race) in the ID field of the Add Organizer dialog.
3. Save the change by clicking OK.

The new location displays in the Sub-Locations table and includes several fields in addition to the location name. The Subs field provides sub-locations assigned to Mill Race. The Devices field lists the total number of devices assigned to the location, and the Events column shows the highest severity event and the number of corresponding number of events. Since we just started, we see all zeros.

We can add as many locations as we need, or we can further define our locations and add sub-locations to the Mill Race organizer. Click on the Mill Race link in the Sub-Locations table. Zenoss now displays information specific to the Mill Race location. Any events that display on the page will be for devices assigned to **/Locations/Mill Race**. Let's add locations for First Floor and Second Floor by selecting the Add New Organizer option from the Sub-Location page menu.

If we click on the First Floor link, we see the status screen that displays information specific to the /Locations/Mill Race/First Floor organizer. Let's go back to the Mill Race location by clicking on Mill Race link in the bread crumbs.

The **Summary** table on the Mill Race **Status** tab contains **Descriptions** and **Address** fields that we can edit. Click on the **Edit** link next to **Description** and enter any number of items, such as driving directions or contacts. Save the changes (refer to the following screenshot).

In order to use the Google Maps portlet, we need to enter a mappable address, such as city and state. Edit the **Address** field and enter the address to pass to Google Maps and click **Save**. Click on the Map tab to display the map view.

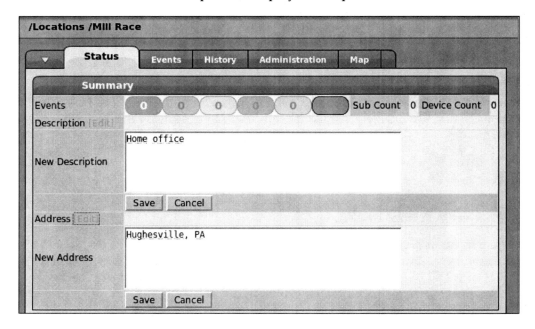

To see multiple locations on the map, add an address for each location; however, you can enter only one address for each location. Click on the Dashboard view and note that the Location portlet now displays a map.

If you followed my examples, then you probably want to remove our test locations and add meaningful locations. To remove a location, select Locations from the navigation bar. Check the box next to Mill Race in the Sub-Locations table. From the Sub-Locations page menu, select Delete Organizers.

Systems And Groups

We continue defining our monitoring environment by setting up system organizers for our example company, which is similar to adding locations. From the navigation panel, select Systems. On the **Systems** screen, Zenoss displays the **Status** tab by default. To add a system organizer:

1. Select Add New Organizer from the Sub-Systems table menu.
2. Type a description (e.g., Support) in the ID field of the Add Organizer dialog.
3. Save the change by clicking OK.
4. Enter a second organizer for **Development**.

The Sub-Systems table displays the newly added **Development** and Support organizers, and each system lists the number of sub-locations, devices, and events (refer to the following screenshot).

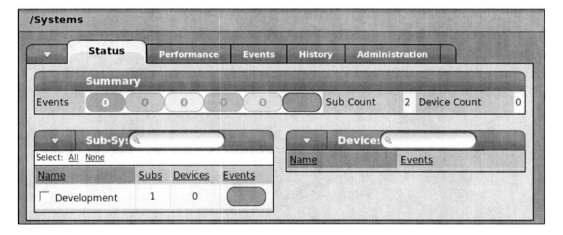

The Systems screen includes tabs for **Performance, Events, History,** and **Administration**. The **Performance** tab displays group performance data. The **Events** tab shows current events for any devices in the organizer, while the **History** tab maintains a list of acknowledged events. The **Administration** tab displays a list of user-defined commands, maintenance windows, and administrators that may be assigned to the Systems organizer. After we add devices to the system, we can assign them to systems and groups.

Next, we'll create a developers group and a software testers group. From the navigation menu, select Groups to display the Groups Status page. To add a system organizer:

1. Select Add New Organizer from the Sub-Groups table menu.
2. Type a description (e.g., Developers) in the ID field of the Add Organizer dialog.
3. Save the change by clicking OK.
4. Enter a second organizer for Software Testers.

The Sub-Groups table displays both groups, but what if we want to classify software testers within the developers group?

No problem. We'll move the groups:

1. Check the box next to **Software Testers** in the **Sub-Groups** menu.
2. Choose **Move Organizers** from the **Sub-Groups** page menu.
3. Select **Developers** from the drop-down list in the **Move Organizers** dialog (refer to the following screenshot).
4. Click **Move**.

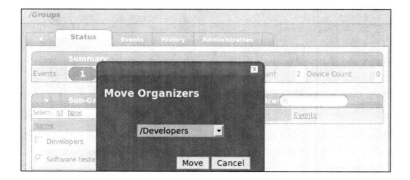

Zenoss refreshes the page and displays the /Groups/Developers group page which now shows the Software Testers sub-group.

Networks

Zenoss can automatically discover all the devices with an IP address on our networks, and if the device responds to an SNMP query, Zenoss adds it to the device inventory. We demonstrate the process of adding devices manually in Chapter 5. We might want to manually add a device to the inventory if our network contains a large amount of devices we do not wish to monitor or if Zenoss did not automatically add the device.

The Mill Race Communications network we use throughout the book is not publicly accessible. Each person should apply network addresses and device names that are specific to their environment in place of the book's examples.

Before we can discover devices, we need to add a network:

1. Select Networks from the navigation panel.
2. Select Add Networks from the Sub-Networks table menu.
3. Enter the IP address (Ex: 192.168.1.1) of the network in the ID field of the Add Network dialog.
4. Click OK.

The following screenshot shows the Networks Overview page:

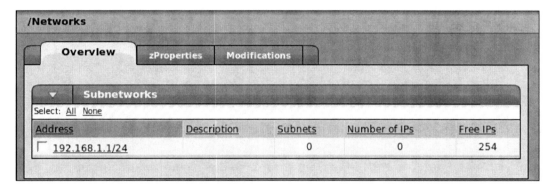

Our new network displays in the **Subnetworks** table. To discover devices:

1. Select the checkbox for the network you want to discover.
2. Select Discover Devices from the Sub-Networks table menu.

Zenoss initiates a ping sweep of the network and looks for active IP addresses. Devices are added to the Discovered device class.

The device discovery process displays a real time log that provides a step-by-step account of the results. The following screenshot shows that Zenoss ran the zendisc command on the network and pinged 254 IP addresses in 51.49 seconds. From those 254 IP addresses, it only found three active IP addresses. The remainder of the log provides some information about each IP address. Obviously, the example uses a small network, but small networks deserve to be monitored too!

Scroll to the bottom of the device discovery log and click on the Navigate to Networks link.

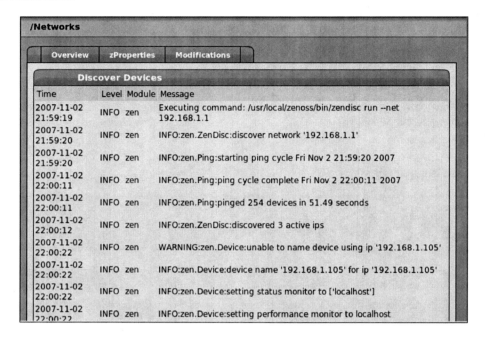

The 192.168.1.1 Sub-network table is now populated with information including subnets, number of IPs, and Free IPs. To view more detailed information, click on the 192.168.1.1 link to navigate to the network's overview page as shown in the following screenshot. The Network table provides an **Overview** of the network, including a user defined description. We can add and discover **Subnetworks** from this page as well.

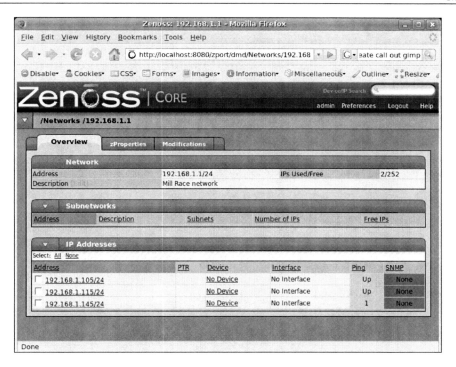

The **IP Addresses** table lists the discovered IPs on the network along with a **Ping** and **SNMP** status.

From the network overview, we get our first look at **zProperties**, which Zenoss uses as a way to define common configuration information for a category of devices. We'll encounter **zProperties** again when we cover the class organizers for events, devices, services, and processes.

The available network zProperties are:

zProperty	Description
zAutoDiscover	Tells zendisc to automatically discover the devices on the network. Enter either true or false.
zDefaultNetworkTree	Lists network subnets in CIDR format. Default values are 24 and 32.
zDrawMapLinks	Tells Google Maps not to draw links for the network. Default value is false. Set to true if you do not use Google Maps or if the network is not at a mappable location.
zIcon	Sets the location of the default network icon.
zPingFailThresh	Enters the number of failed ping requests Zenoss processes before the device is removed. Default value is 168.

Inheritance

Our discussion about Network zProperties introduces an opportune time to talk about inheritance in Zenoss. Inheritance means that devices assume the configuration of its parent organizers and often go from general to specific. We'll demonstrate inheritance using networks.

From the navigation panel, select Networks. Our test company has at least one network added to Zenoss already; let's add a second network. We'll use 192.168.2.0 for our example. Our list of networks now contains 192.168.1.1 and 192.168.2.0, which translates into the following hierarchies:

- /Networks/192.168.1.1
- /Networks/192.168.2.0

For our test, we'll make configuration changes at the network organizer level and to the individual 192.168.1.1 network:

1. At the Network level, select **zProperties**.
2. Set **zAutoDiscover** to false and save.
3. Select the **Overview** tab to display the list of networks.
4. Follow the 192.168.1.1 network link.
5. Select the **zProperties** tab from the 192.168.1.1 Networks Overview page.
6. Set **zAutoDiscover** to true and save (refer to the following screenshot).
7. Go back to the Network level to display the list of all networks.

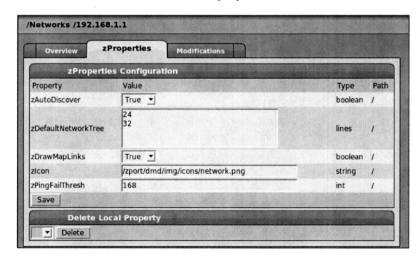

At this point, we have a custom configuration. The 192.168.1.1 network inherits the properties of its parent network organizer, with one exception. On the 192.168.1.1 network, we will be able to automatically discover devices because we set the **zAutoDiscover** to "**true**."

To test our network inheritance setup, select the checkbox for both the 192.168.1.1 and 192.168.2.0 networks from the Sub-Networks list. From the table menu, select Discover.

Zenoss runs the zendisc command and displays the results in the Discover Devices summary window. You can review the scan results. Even though we tried to discover devices on both networks, Zenoss did not poll the 192.168.2.0 network because it inherited the Networks zProperties, which disables device auto-discovery. However, Zenoss did discover the devices on the 192.168.1.1 network because we gave 192.168.1.1 a custom auto-discovery property.

Classes

Several classes exist to organize devices, events, services, and processes based on common groupings, but we'll stick to talking about devices in this chapter. For example, the devices we discovered on our network are automatically classified as discovered. At this point, you may be remembering our discussion about the Browse By Organizers and wonder in just how many ways we can categorize items.

The organizers we use for locations, systems, and groups do not affect how we monitor devices. They provide a logistical overview of our monitoring environment, but our devices do not inherit any configuration properties from them.

Classes, however, do affect how we monitor devices. Each device class has configurable zProperties, which means that the devices we add to /Server/Linux inherit a common configuration. It also means that they share monitoring properties with all devices classified under the server hierarchy and Linux classes. As we did with networks, we can also set zProperties for individual devices.

We need to change the classification of the devices Zenoss auto-discovered from the default Discovered class to something more descriptive. Select Devices from the navigation panel.

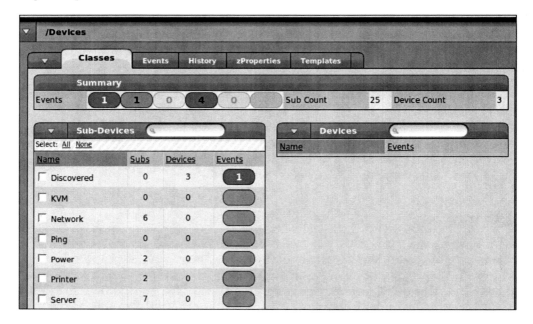

The first thing we notice when the **Device** page loads (as shown in the previous screenshot)is the row of tabs—**Classes, Events, History, zProperties,** and **Templates.** The **Classes** tab shows an overview of the current organizer and opens by default. The **Events** tab shows all the events for all the devices that are members of the class. Likewise, the **History** tab shows the past events for all the devices in the class. We discussed **zProperties** before and we will see them again. The **Templates** tab lists the available performance templates for the class. How Zenoss collects and displays performance data can be customized using templates, and like zProperties, devices inherit the templates of their class.

The next field we see on the Device Class section is the **Summary** table. The table lists the number of **Events,** by severity, for the class. It also displays a summary total of all sub-classes and the number of devices contained in the class.

The **Sub-Devices** table displays a list of classes available to the selected class. For each class in the list, Zenoss provides summary information that includes the number of **Sub-classes, Devices,** and **Events.**

Zenoss provides the following class hierarchies in the **Sub-Devices** table:

- **Discovered**
- **KVM**
- **Network**
  - Router
    - Cisco
    - Firewall
    - RSM
    - TerminalServer
  - Switch
- **Ping**
- **Power**
  - UPS
    - APC
- **Printer**
  - InkJet
  - Laser
- **Server**
  - Cmd
  - Darwin
  - Linux
  - Remote
  - Scan
  - Solaris

In this chapter, we use classes as a way to establish device relationships. In Chapter 5, we use classes as the basis for our modeling exercise because the information Zenoss provides us about a device is determined, in part, by its class association.

Set Device Properties

The Devices table, which is adjacent to the Sub-Devices table, lists all the devices for the selected class. We do not have any devices assigned to the top-level devices organizer, so the device list is blank. To display a list of devices for the Discovered class, click on the Discovered link in the Sub-Devices table.

Now we are viewing the **/Devices/Discovered** class and the bread crumb navigation confirms our location in the hierarchy. In the following screen capture, we see three devices associated with the Discovered class, but we want to change that.

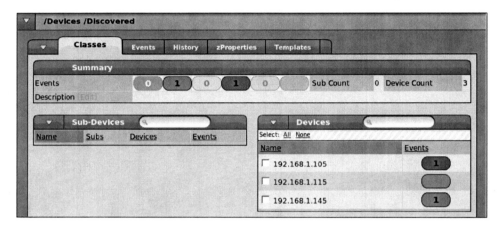

When we click on the Devices page menu, we get our first look at several device management functions. The following table lists the options and a brief description.

Menu	Description
Set Production State	Available production states are production, pre-production, test, maintenance, and decommissioned.
	The production state affects the monitoring and alerting status of the device.
Set Priority	Available priorities are highest, high, normal, low, lowest, and trivial.
Move to Class	Assigns a class organizer.
Set Groups	Assigns a group organizer.
Set Systems	Assigns a system organizer.
Set Location	Assigns a location.
Set Status Monitors	Assigns a status monitor to define how Zenoss polls the device.

Menu	Description
Set Perf Monitors	Assign a performance monitor to define how Zenoss collects performance data for the device.
Delete Devices	Remove the selected device.
Lock Devices	Prevent the device from being removed if the device is not active during network auto discovery.

Right now, we want to assign class, group, system, and location to our devices. We'll continue using devices specific to Mill Race Communications in the examples, but if you have already discovered your own devices, substitute values as needed.

First, assign locations:

1. Click the 192.168.1.145 and 192.168.1.105 devices to select them.
2. From the Devices page menu, select Set Location.
3. Select /Mill Race/Second Floor from the Set Location dialog; click OK.
4. Assign the 192.168.1.115 device to the /Mill Race location.

Second, assign groups:

1. Select all the devices from the Devices table. We can mass select all the devices in the list by clicking on the "All" select link located in the second row of the Devices table.
2. From the page menu, select Set Groups.
3. Select /Developers/Software Testers from the Set Groups dialog; click OK.

Third, assign systems:

1. Select 192.168.1.115 from the device list.
2. From the page menu, select Systems.
3. Select /Developers from the Set Systems dialog; click OK.

Fourth, assign classes:

1. Select 192.168.1.115 from the device list.
2. From the page menu, select Move Classes.
3. Select /Server/Linux from the Move Classes dialog; click OK.

Whoa! The screen has changed. Let's take a moment and see if we can figure out where we are. Look at the bread crumb navigation. Zenoss opens the new device class when we move classes, which means we are looking at the /Server/Linux page. We still have a few assignments to make, so go back to the /Devices/ Discovered class.

We finish our device assignments by moving the device 192.168.1.145 to the /Server/ Darwin class and the device 192.168.1.105 to the /Printer class.

Now that we have defined our device relationships, let's take a quick tour around the application to see how our changes fit into the system. When we select Groups from the navigation panel, we see Zenoss displays three devices for the Developers group. If we click on the Developers sub-group, we see the Software Testers group with three devices listed. Follow the Software Testers link to display all three of our sample devices.

Next, select Locations from the navigation panel and follow the Mill Race link. Here we see the device 192.168.1.115 assigned to the Mill Race location, but the other devices are further classified under the Second Floor location.

Summary

While speaking about two key concepts, hierarchy and inheritance, we got the firsthand experience of navigating the Zenoss web application and were able to start our device inventory. If you haven't already done so, apply the information in this chapter to your own network so that you can facilitate the way you manage your devices.

In Chapter 5, we continue discussing our device management concepts by adding more devices manually, and we'll model our devices with SSH and SNMP. We also take an in-depth look at the Device List view.

5
Device Management

Based on the work done in Chapter 4, Zenoss is now monitoring all the devices we automatically added to our inventory and if we look around the web interface, we may notice that some devices have events associated with them. At any moment, we can get the up/down status for each device, but we'll to continue to build a more detailed model of our networks.

We'll start this chapter by fine -tuning our device inventory through manually adding devices to our inventory. Then we'll take a look at the main device status view and perform some routine device administration tasks. The second half of the chapter demonstrates the available monitoring protocols that Zenoss uses to model the devices. Device modeling builds relationships between devices and inventories the services, processes, and hardware on each device.

We'll continue to demonstrate features using the Mill Race network, but feel free to substitute your own devices in the examples given in this chapter. By the time we finish Chapter 5, we'll have a detailed model of our networks that we will continue to build upon in later chapters.

Add Devices

In Chapter 4, we auto-discovered the devices on our networks, but sometimes we don't want to add all the available devices on the network to the inventory or it may be that all our devices may not be found. To compensate for both these scenarios, Zenoss allows us to add one device at a time to the device inventory.

To add a single device, select **Add Device** from the navigation panel. The **Add Device** page is divided into multiple sections for general device information, **Attributes**, and **Relations** as shown in the following screenshot. We can be as detailed as we want to be when we add the device manually. However, at a minimum, we should enter a **Device Name**, **Device Class Path**, and **Discovery Protocol**.

The **Device Name** identifies the IP address or resolvable hostname, while the device class sets the monitoring properties we want our device to inherit by default. If the device is not SNMP-enabled, select **None**, otherwise Zenoss will not add the device.

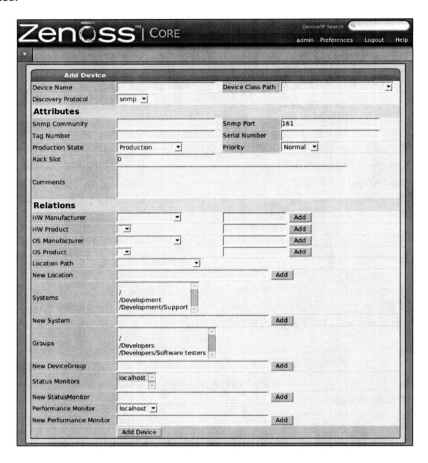

We'll continue monitoring our Mill Race location by adding a new Linux server with the following configuration:

Device Name: 192.168.1.110

Device Class: /Server/Linux

Discovery Protocol: None

OS Manufacturer: Ubuntu

Location: /Mill Race/Second Floor

System: /Development

Group: /Developers/Software Testers

The **Add Device Options** table lists the available configuration information we can set when adding a device manually.

Add Device Options

Field Name	Description
Device Name	Enter either an IP address or resolvable host name to identify the device.
Device Class Path	Select the appropriate device classifications: For example: /Server/Linux.
Discovery Protocol	Choose either SNMP or None depending on whether or not you monitor the device with SNMP.
SNMP Community	Enter the community string of the device. The most common default is public.
Attributes	
SNMP Port	The default port for SNMP communication is 161.
Tag Number	If the device has a tag number, such as a service tag number, enter the value.
Serial Number	Record the manufacturer's serial number.
Production State	Select the current state of the device: For example: Production, maintenance, decommissioned.
Priority	Highest, high, normal, low, lowest, trivial.
Rack Slot	Record the physical rack location of the device.
Comments	Use the comments to enter device-specific information, including description, device users, or who is responsible for the device.
Relations	
HW Manufacturer	Select a manufacturer name from the list. For example: Cisco or Linksys.
HW Product	Select a product from the list. The HW Product lists gets populated based on the HW Manufacturer selection.
OS Manufacturer	Select a manufacturer name from the list. For example: Microsoft or Fedora Core.

Add Device Options

Field Name	Description
OS Product	Select a product from the list. The OS Product list gets populated based on the HW Manufacturer selection.
Location Path	Select the location of the device. Create a new location by typing the name in the New Location field and clicking Add.
Systems	Select a system organizer. Create a new system by typing the name in the New System field and clicking Add.
Groups	Select a group organizer. Create a new group by typing the name in the New Device Group field and clicking Add.
Status Monitor	Select a status monitor to define how often the device availability is monitored. The default is localhost. Create a new status monitor by typing the name in the New Status Monitor field and clicking Add. Refer to Chapter 6 for configuration information.
Performance Monitor	Select a performance monitor to define how often device performance data is collected. The default is localhost. Create a new performance monitor by typing the name in the New Performance Monitor field. Refer to Chapter 6 for configuration information.

After we enter the configuration information for the device, click the Add button. If Zenoss encounters an error while adding the device, the error will be printed in the status window. Check the add device properties and try again. If Zenoss successfully adds the device, the **Status** window displays a log indicating device's properties as shown in the following screenshot.

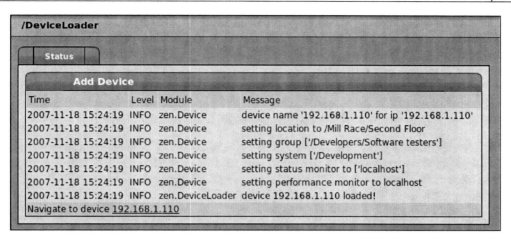

The Add Device Status page provides a hyperlink at the bottom of the page that says, "**Navigate to device 192.168.1.110**." If we click on the device name, the Device Status page is displayed.

Device Status

The Device status page displays an overview of our device and contains the same information we encountered on the Add Device page. As we look at the **Device Status** table for 192.168.1.110 as shown in the following screenshot, we can determine several important monitoring statistics in one glance.

In our example, the device name and IP address are the same, but they do not need to be the same. If the host has multiple CNAMEs or interfaces, we can specify a name other than the name we used to find the device, via DNS resolution. We may find that we want to implement a custom naming scheme for devices. Regardless of what we name the device, Zenoss uses the IP address to monitor, not the name.

The **Device Status** table lists the number of events by severity and color code. The Device Severities table lists Zenoss's severity:

Device Severities	
Color	**Severity**
Red	Critical
Orange	Error
Yellow	Warning
Blue	Information
Grey	Debug

The **Device Status** page also lists important statistics of the device. The **Availability** and **Uptime** values are automatically calculated, and the **Production State** and **Priority** values can be changed via the device's Edit page. We can lock the device to prevent Zenoss from removing or updating the device configuration. The **Last Change**, **Last Collection**, and the **First Seen** values provide a quick way to verify the modeling history of the device by listing the last time Zenoss detected a change with the device configuration and the last time the device was modeled.

In the **Device Status** page, we also see a list of **Component Types** and the **Status** of each monitored component. As we build our monitoring solution, the components we monitor will change per device, but common components include SNMP, ipServices, Windows event logs, and syslogs.

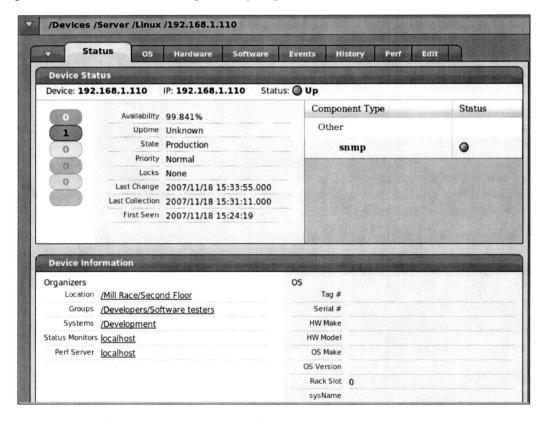

If we look closely at the previous screen shot that shows the status of 192.168.1.110, we notice that the SNMP component displays an error condition. This indicates that our device does not have SNMP installed or is not configured correctly. Refer to the Server Setup section in Chapter 3 for help in SNMP configuration.

Up to this point, we have only added devices to our inventory, so why do we see an error message for SNMP anyway? When we added the device, we set the class /Server/Linux, which implies that the device uses the modeling properties defined in the class. The /Server/Linux class uses the SNMP monitoring by default. We'll talk more about modeling our devices in the modeling section of this chapter.

Like other pages, Zenoss provides context-aware menus that allow us to manage our device from the Device Status page. When we click on the page menu, three submenus display: **More**, **Manage**, and **Run Commands**. As we work through this chapter, we will cover many of the available menu options, but the following series of screen shots provide a quick view of each menu.

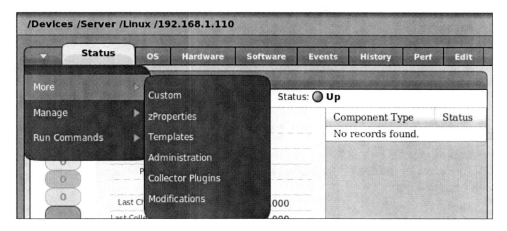

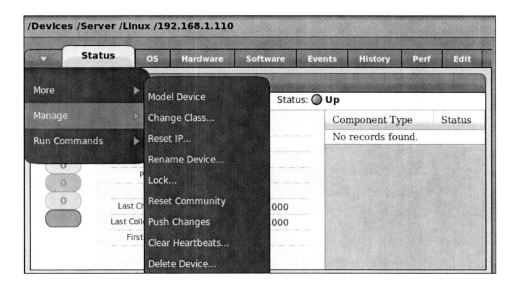

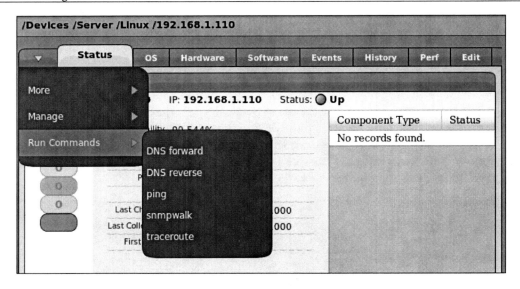

Device Administration

From the page menu on the Device Status page, we can perform several administration-related tasks, including reset IP address, rename, and lock the device configuration.

Lock Or Unlock Device

Zenoss automatically polls the devices in our inventory and remodels the devices when it finds changes. We can lock the device's configuration from being updated by Zenoss. We can also lock the device from being deleted from the inventory.

To change the lock status of a device:

1. From the **Device Status** page menu, select **Manage > Lock**.
2. Select from the following choices as shown in the following screenshot:
   ° **Send event when actions are blocked by a lock**
   ° **Lock from deletion and updates**
   ° **Lock from deletion**
   ° **Unlock**
3. The device status page displays after we choose a locking option.

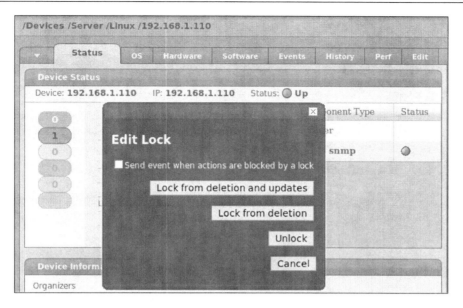

If we lock the device, the lock status displays a padlock icon on the Device Status page.

Rename A Device

Zenoss automatically detects and populates the device name, but we can name the device as anything we want. We'll change the name of our 192.1.168.110 device:

1. From **Device Status** page menu, select **Manage** > **Rename** Device.
2. Enter the new name (e.g., Coyote) in the ID field of the Rename Device dialog.
3. Click **OK** to save the change.

On the **Device Status** page, the device information updates to reflect the new name, **Coyote** as shown in the following screenshot. Even the breadcrumb navigation changes to reflect the name.

The device name will not be updated by the Zenoss modeling process.

Reset IP Address

If the IP address of a device changes, we need to update Zenoss to reflect the correct configuration. To change the IP address of our newly named Coyote:

1. From Device Status page menu, select **Manage > Reset IP**.

2. Enter the new resolvable host name or IP address in the IP field of the **Reset IP** dialog box (shown in the following screenshot) or leave it blank to allow Zenoss to lookup the IP based on the device name.

3. Click **OK** to save the change.

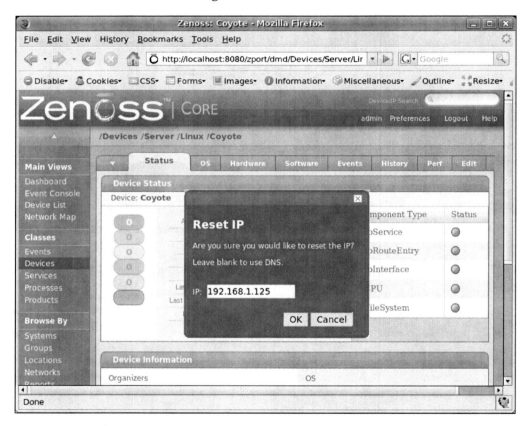

Push Changes

After we make changes to the device, we can "push" the changes live right away instead of waiting for Zenoss to remodel the device. From the Device Status page menu, select Manage > Push Changes. Zenoss confirms the action with a status message as shown in the following screenshot.

Device List

Up to this point, we have been administering our devices on a per device level, which is acceptable if we only want to make a few changes to one or two devices. If we want to mass update our device properties, we use the **Device List** view.

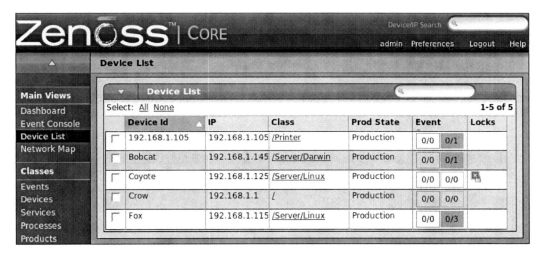

To display a list of devices, select **Device List** from the navigation panel (Device List is shown in the previous screenshot).

The **Device List** table divides into columns for **Device ID, IP, Class, Production State, Event,** and **Locks,** which provides succinct synopsis of the state of our devices.

The device names and classes are hyperlinks that take you to the device's status page and the class' summary pages. The **Event** page displays two squares per device. The squares with the red borders display the critical events, and the squares with no borders display error events. **Events** are listed as the number of acknowledged events over the total number of events.

If we have a large inventory, selecting a device from a list of entries becomes cumbersome, so we can sort the table by **Device ID, IP, Class,** or **Production State.** Click on the column heading to change the sort order and note the white triangle that shows whether the column is sorted in ascending or descending order. Click the column heading again to reverse the sort order.

If we know the name of the device we want to find, Zenoss provides a global search box that we can use to search by device name or IP. The **Device/IP Search** box is right-aligned at the top of the page and to the right of the Zenoss Core logo.

If Zenoss finds a device matching the search criteria, it automatically opens the Device Status page. If multiple devices match the search criteria, Zenoss displays a search results page, so that we can select the correct device.

The **Device List** table also has a search box, but it's more flexible and allows us to search by the **Device Name**, **IP**, **Production State**, and **Class**. As an example, enter the search term "**linux**" and press enter. The list of devices changes to reflect all devices that contain Linux in the name, **Production State**, or **Class** (as shown in the following screenshot).

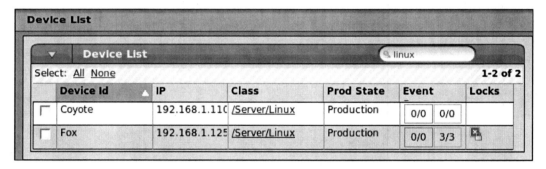

The **Device List** view not only displays the list of devices, it also allows us to mass update a group of devices by setting properties such as class, groups, locations, status monitors, performance monitors, and production states.

Let's walk through a quick example and change the location for all our devices:

1   Select **All** devices in the list.
2   From the page menu, select Set Location.
3   From the **Set Location** dialog box, choose a new location (for example, **Mill Race**).
4   Click the **Set Location** button.

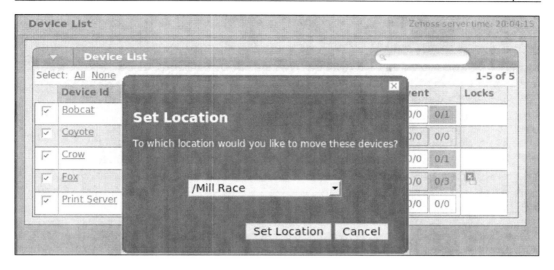

This process eliminates the sub-locations that we set in our initial configuration in Chapter 4 and all the devices are now assigned to Mill Race.

Delete Devices

If we physically remove a device from our network, we need to update our Zenoss inventory. Otherwise, Zenoss will continue to monitor a device that no longer exists. We can either set the device's production state to decommissioned or delete the device from the Device List. If we change the production state to decommissioned, the device still displays in the Device List, but Zenoss no longer monitors it.

We remove devices from our inventory from the Device List view with just a few steps:

1   Select the device from the list.
2   From the page menu, select **Delete** Devices.
3   Click **OK** to confirm the delete.

The device will no longer show in inventory and Zenoss will not monitor or model it. However, removing the device from the Device List does not remove the performance data associated with the device. If we add the same device name back into Zenoss, the existing performance data will be available. Zenoss stores the performance data by device name in $ZENHOME/perf.

Model Devices

When we talk about Zenoss, two related but different words often come up, monitoring and modeling. Monitoring refers to the availability of the device and answers the question, "Is the device accessible?" Modeling defines a relationship between devices and identifies the components available on a device, such as services, interfaces, and file systems.

Zenoss models devices via SNMP, SSH, port scan, and telnet and gathers information via collector plug-ins. Each class has a default set of collector plug-ins that tells Zenoss how to model the devices assigned to the class. We can add or remove collector plug-ins at the device level for individual changes or at the class level for all the devices in the class.

The collector plug-in names reflect the monitoring protocol they are used for. All the SNMP collectors contain "snmp" in the name. The SSH and telnet plug-in names contain "cmd," and the port scan plug-in contains "portscan" in the name.

We'll step through modeling examples for SNMP, SSH, and port scan; however, we'll skip telnet because it's similar to SSH.

SNMP

Zenoss defaults to SNMP monitoring, and as we discussed in Chapter 3, the monitored device needs to have SNMP installed and configured to work properly. If you glossed over the SNMP configuration in Chapter 3, take a moment to review the information now.

Zenoss supports SNMP v1, v2c, and v3. The example commands used in this section to troubleshoot SNMP specify v1.

Test SNMP

If we're unsure of our SNMP setup, we can test it by running the snmpwalk command to retrieve the values of the MIB tree on the monitored device. We'll demonstrate both working and broken SNMP configurations on the Mill Race network.

From the Device List, select the device named Coyote. From the Device Status page menu, choose **Run Commands > snmpwalk**. A new window opens and we see the results of the snmpwalk command as shown in the following screenshot.

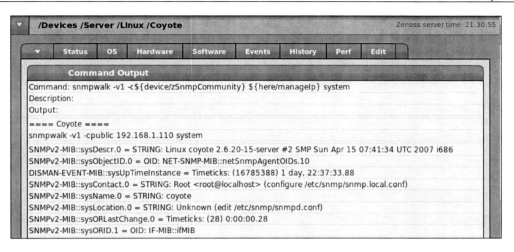

Now we select the device Bobcat from the Device List view. Run the snmpwalk command from the Device Status page. This time, we receive a **Timeout** error, which indicates that we have a problem with SNMP on the device Bobcat as shown in the following screenshot.

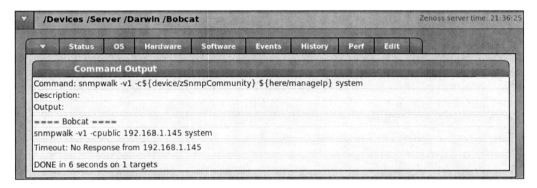

Assuming that SNMP is properly configured on the device and that the monitored device accepts traffic on port 161, we may need to update the device's community string. To update the community:

1   Select the device from the Device List view.
2   From the Device Status page menu, select More > zProperties.
3   Find the Community field and enter the correct value.
4   Save the changes.

After updating the SNMP community string in the zProperties, we run the snmpwalk command again to see if we have fixed the problem.

If we continue to encounter problems getting Zenoss to model a device with SNMP, we can try to narrow down the problem by running the following `snmpwalk` command from the monitored devices shell prompt:

```
snmpwalk -v1 -c public localhost system
```

Replace `public` with the correct community string. If the command is successful when using localhost, edit the snmpd configuration file. As root, edit `/etc/default/snmpd` or `/etc/default/snmp` and remove `127.0.0.1` from the following line:

```
SNMPDPORTS = '-Lsd -Lf /dev/null -u snmp -I -smux -p /var/run/snmpd.
pid 127.0.0.1'
```

After editing the `/etc/default/snmpd` file, restart the snmpd service as root. For example:

```
/etc/init.d/snmpd stop
```

```
/etc/init.d/snmpd start
```

Retest the `snmpwalk` command to confirm that SNMP is working correctly. Windows users can run `wbemtest` from the command line as outlined in Chapter 3 to test SNMP. If problems remain, consult chapter 11 for a list of Zenoss Core community help resources.

Windows Considerations

The Windows SNMP installation is covered in the Server Setup section of Chapter 3, but in order to collect information from WMI, we need to configure the zProperties for the Windows device. Navigate to the Windows device and open the zProperties page by selecting the **More** > **zProperties** from the page menu. Scroll to the bottom of the page and make the following changes:

- Set zWinEventLog to true.
- Enter the Windows user's password in the zWinPassword field.
- Enter the user name with administrative rights in the zWinUser field in the following formats:
    - `.\user` for local user accounts
    - `DOMAIN\user` for domain user accounts
- Set zWMIMonitorIgnore to false.

Save the changes, and Zenoss is ready to model the information on the Windows device. We can force a model by selecting **Manage** > **Model Device** from the page menu.

SNMP Collector Plug-ins

The Collector Plug-ins assigned to the device determine how Zenoss models the device. Let's take a look at our example device Coyote and see what collectors are currently assigned. From the Device Status page for Coyote, select More > Collector Plug-ins from the page menu.

A page showing the assigned collector plugi-ns displays in the left column of the page with an Add Fields link on the right. When we click on the Add Fields link, a column of unassigned plug-ins appears and the link name changes to **Hide Fields** as shown in the following screenshot.

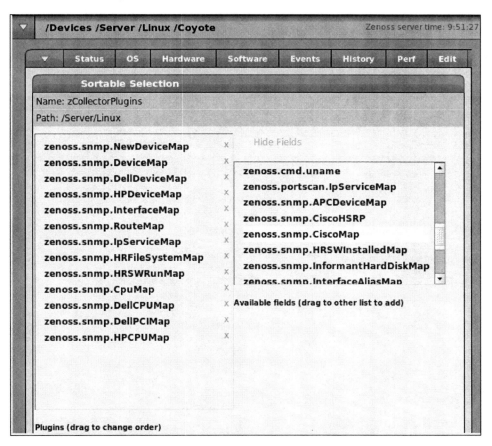

The plug-in names are intuitive in that the name suggests the type of information we expect to be modeling. For example, `zenoss.snmp.IpServiceMap` returns a list of active IP services on the device, such as HTTP. The Dell specific plugi-ns retrieve more detailed information from Dell devices using OpenManage, and the HP plugi-ns provide more information about devices using Insight Management agents.

To remove a plug-in from the assigned plug-in list, click on the "**x**" next to the plug-in name. To assign a plug-in, drag the plug-in name from available list to the assigned list.

To see how our devices are affected, let's remove the **zenoss.snmp.IpServiceMap** and add `zenoss.cmd.df`. After we make the changes to the plug-ins for Coyote, scroll to the bottom of the page and click Save.

Model Device

Zenoss automatically models each device in our inventory every six hours, but we can manually force Zenoss to model the device. From the Device Status page, select **Manage** > **Model Device** from the page menu.

Zenoss displays the results of the `zenmodeler` command in the window as shown in the following screenshot.

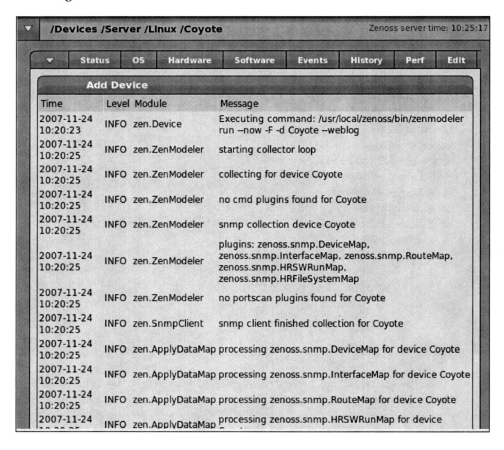

Zenoss first determines which plugi-ns are available and then collects information based on those plug-ins. Notice that no cmd plug-ins are found, which means that the `zenoss.cmd.df` plug-in we added to Coyote will not be collected. After Zenoss models the device, we can review the device overview page to see what component types Zenoss discovered. IpService should not be listed.

If we go back to the Collector Plug-ins page for Coyote, we can add the `zenoss.snmp.IpService` plug-in and then model the device again. Now, **IpServices** is displayed in the **Component Type** list as shown in the following screenshot.

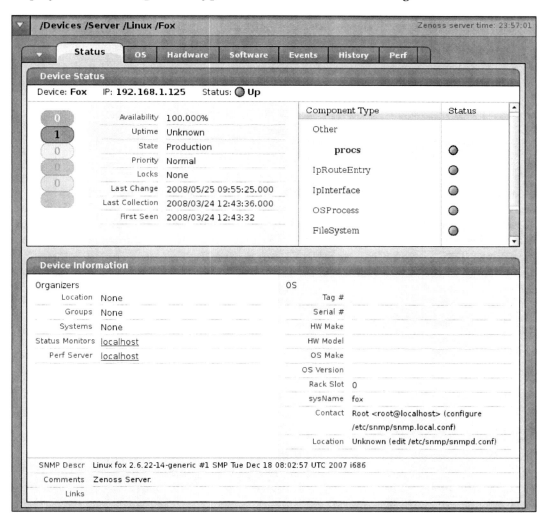

The **Component Type** list gets updated as part of the modeling process and so does the **OS** fields in the **Device Information** table (the greyed-out fields in the screen shot). If we enter values in these fields during the Add Device step, the values would be overwritten with the SNMP values.

Our example made changes to the device level, which means that if we view the collector plug-ins for the /Server/Linux device class, the original plug-ins are specified. To view the plug-ins for the class:

1   Select **Devices** from the navigation panel.

2   Select **Server** from the sub-devices list.

3   Select **Linux** from the sub-devices list.

4   From the /Devices/Server/Linux page menu, select **More > Collector Plug-ins**.

Devices automatically inherit any changes we make to the class collector plug-ins the next time Zenoss models the devices.

SSH Modeling

If the monitored device does not support SNMP, or if we need to monitor a device behind a firewall, SSH provides an alternative to SNMP. Unlike SNMP, SSH needs the Zenoss Plug-ins installed on each monitored device and platform support is limited to Linux, Darwin, and FreeBSD. We also need to make sure that the monitored device has an SSH server installed so that the Zenoss system can log in and retrieve information. OpenSSH from openssh.com offers a good cross-platform SSH solution.

The level of modeling provided by the Zenoss Plug-ins varies between platforms. For this reason, we may not achieve the same level of detail as we do with SNMP, but SSH modeling provides more detail than a port scan.

To help us setup our SSH monitoring, Zenoss provides the /Server/Cmd class which is already configured with the command plug-ins we need to monitor via SSH.

SSH Collector Plug-ins

From the navigation panel, select **Devices**. Navigate to the /Server/Cmd class and click on the **zProperties** tab. Find the zCollectorPlug-ins field and click on the **Edit** link. A list of the assigned collector plug-ins is displayed as shown in the following screenshot.

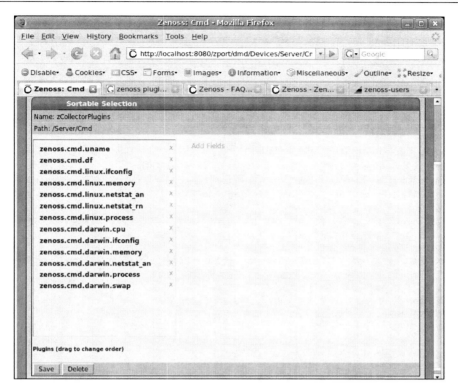

The important thing to note with the command collector plug-ins is the new level of specificity in the name. The **zenoss.cmd.uname** and **zenoss.cmd.df** plug-ins are common to all architectures, while the plug-ins with "linux" in the name work with Linux systems. Mac OS X platforms use the plug-ins with "darwin" in the name.

If we did not have any any OS X systems to monitor, then we could remove all the Darwin-based plug-ins from the /Server/Cmd class or, if we know that we don't want to monitor the memory usage for any of our devices, we can remove that plug-in.

We'll leave the collector plug-ins as they are for the **/Server/Cmd** class and change our test device Coyote to use SSH instead of SNMP.

Zenoss Plug-ins

Zenoss will monitor and retrieve some data using the SSH modeler even if we do not install the Zenoss plug-ins, but the device model will be incomplete. For example, file systems will be detected along with the size of each drive., but the usage statistics will not be reported. Zenoss also generates warning events if it cannot find the `zenplugin.py` command on the monitored system.

The monitored system needs a Python environment installed. This can be installed using your distribution's package manager. If you have setuptools installed, you can install the Zenoss-Plug-ins package from the Cheese Shop (http://pypi.python.org/pypi/) with the following command as root:

```
easy_install Zenoss-Plugins
```

```
mike@coyote:~$ sudo easy_install Zenoss-Plugins
Password:
Searching for Zenoss-Plugins
Reading http://cheeseshop.python.org/pypi/Zenoss-Plugins/
Reading http://www.zenoss.com
Reading http://cheeseshop.python.org/pypi/Zenoss-Plugins/1.0.0
Best match: Zenoss-Plugins 1.0.0
Downloading http://pypi.python.org/packages/source/Z/Zenoss-Plugins/Zenoss-Plug
ins-1.0.0.tar.gz#md5=a427fded3e5504a1c9e14d7571778927
Processing Zenoss-Plugins-1.0.0.tar.gz
Running Zenoss-Plugins-1.0.0/setup.py -q bdist_egg --dist-dir /tmp/easy_install
-fKrxZc/Zenoss-Plugins-1.0.0/egg-dist-tmp-mnIB0G
zip_safe flag not set; analyzing archive contents...
Adding Zenoss-Plugins 1.0.0 to easy-install.pth file
Installing zenplugin.py script to /usr/bin

Installed /usr/lib/python2.5/site-packages/Zenoss_Plugins-1.0.0-py2.5.egg
Processing dependencies for Zenoss-Plugins
mike@coyote:~$
```

We can also build the Zenoss Plug-ins package from source:

1   Download the Zenoss Plug-ins package from
    http://www.zenoss.com/download/.

2   Extract the plug-in file.

3   From the plug-in source directory, run the following commands as root:

    ○   python setup.py build

    ○   python setup.py install

The setuptools procedure installs zenplugin.py to /usr/bin, which is important because we need to configure the device zProperties to look for the plug-ins in the correct location.

To ensure that the plug-in file is working correctly, run the following command on the monitored device, which is Coyote in our example:

```
zenplugin.py -list-plugins
```

The command outputs the detected platform and the supported plug-ins as shown in the following screenshot.

```
mike@coyote:~$ zenplugin.py --list-plugin
platform 'linux2' supports the following plugins:
  process
  mem
  disk
  cpu
  io
mike@coyote:~$ 
```

Model Device

In order to get Zenoss to model Coyote, we need to tell Zenoss how to connect. First, we'll change the class to /Server/Cmd because it's already configured with the plug-ins we need to use. Second, we'll configure the zProperties so that Zenoss can log in to the device and run system commands.

Navigate to Coyote's Device Status page, and from the page menu, select **Manage** > **Change Class**. Select /Server/Cmd and confirm the selection by clicking **OK**.

Next open the zProperties. From the page menu, select **More** > **zProperties**. Make the following changes:

- Set zCommandUsername to the SSH login on the monitored device.
- Set the user's password in zCommandPassword.
- Change zCommandPath to /usr/bin.
- Set zSnmpMonitorIgnore to true.

When we type the password in zCommandPassword, it will be in clear text, but after we save the zProperties, the password will be starred out. After we have all the changes entered, click **Save**.

Find the zCollectorPlug-ins field and click on the **Edit** link to display the collector plug-ins page. Verify the plug-ins listed are for the /Server/Cmd class only. If not, remove the SNMP plug-ins and add the cmd plug-ins. Save any changes.

Now, let's model the device. From the page menu, select **Manage > Model Device**.

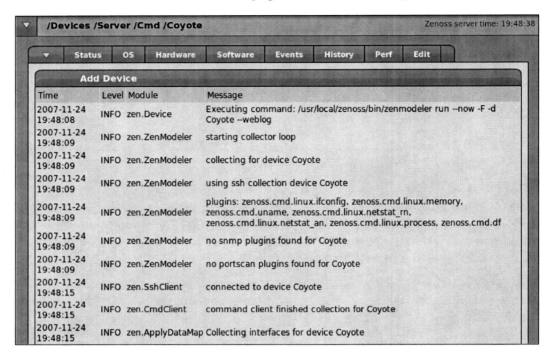

The modeling process resembles the process for SNMP, but notice that this time we're using the cmd plug-ins instead of the SNMP.

Port Scan Modeling

Sometimes, the only option we have to model our devices is with a port scan. A port scan tries to guess which services are running on a device by connecting to various ports. Port scans provide the least detailed model and may raise security alerts on your network. Consult the security administrators before port scanning devices on the network.

Zenoss creates a separate device class in /Server/Scan to handle these devices. There is only one plug-in available, and it is named zenoss.portscan.IpServiceMap. As the name implies, it returns a list of services running on the device.

We go through the same steps to model a device with port scan as we do for SNMP and SSH.

OS Tab

After Zenoss models the devices, it populates the operating system (OS) tab with its findings. From the device's Status page, click on the **OS** tab.

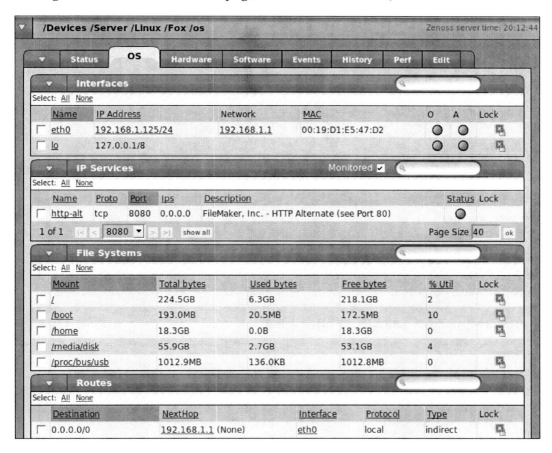

We'll discuss each of the sections in more detail in Chapter 6, but we see that Zenoss has detected the **Interfaces**, **IP Services**, **File Systems**, and **Routes** for our server, **Fox** as shown in the previous screenshot. Those groupings should sound familiar, as we've seen various implementations of those collector plug-ins for SNMP and SSH plug-ins.

Hardware Tab

With the exception of the port scan, the Zenoss models include information about a device's memory and CPU. We can access the Hardware tab by clicking the tab labeled **Hardware** from the Device Status page.

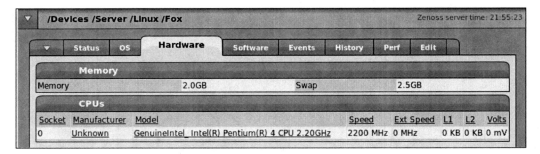

If we monitor a Windows system, we can gather hard disk information by adding the `zenoss.snmp.InformantHardDiskMap` collector plug-in to the device.

Device zProperties

In the course of the chapter, we have changed several zProperties at the device or class level to define how we monitor our devices. The following table lists the available zProperties and a description of each.

zProperty	Description
zCollectorClientTimeout	Set the timeout of the client collector in seconds. The default is 180.
zCollectorDecoding	Specify the character encoding. The default is latin-1.
zCollectorLogChanges	Set to true to log changes and false not to log changes to the collector.
zCollectorPlug-ins	Click the Edit link to open the collector plug-in selection page.
zCommandCommandTimeout	Time in seconds to wait for a command to finish. The default is 15.
zCommandCycleTime	Specifies a time in seconds to cycle through zCommands. The default is 60.
zCommandExistanceTest	Test to see if a command exists on the monitored device. The default is 'test -f %s'.
zCommandLoginTimeout	Wait for the specified seconds for a login prompt. The default is 10.

zProperty	Description
zCommandLoginTries	Attempt to log in the number of specified times. The default is 1.
zCommandPassword	Enter the password for the user's shell account on the monitored device.
zCommandPath	Enter the path of the `zenplugin.py` command. The default is `/opt/zenoss/libexec`; however, the default installation path for `zenplugin.py` is `/usr/bin`
zCommandPort	The port the monitored system uses for SSH connections. The default is 22.
zCommandProtocol	Specify the protocol (telnet, ssh) to use. The default is SSH.
zCommandSearchPath	Specify all the paths to search for the commands.
zCommandUsername	Enter the user log in name for the monitored device.
zDeviceTemplates	Enter the templates by name to use to display information. The default is device.
zFileSystemMapIgnoreNames	Enter the names of the files system to ignore. For example: `/boot`.
zIcon	Each device class has a default icon that can be changed as necessary.
zIfDescription	Displays the interface description on the Interfaces table of the OS tab. Select either true or false. The default is false.
zInterfaceMapIgnoreNames	Enter the names of the interfaces to ignore. For example: lo.
zInterfaceMapIgnoreTypes	Enter the type of interfaces to ignore. For example: local loopback.
zIpServiceMapMaxPort	Specify the maximum port number to port scan. The default is 1024.
zKeyPath	Specify the path to the user's public key file for use with public-key authentication.
zLinks	Enter HTML markup or TALES expressions to display a link for the device. For example, you can create a link to a router's administration console that will display on the Device Status page.

zProperty	Description
zLocalInterfaceNames	A regular expression match to identify local interface names. The default expression looks for lo (loopback) and vmnet (Vmware).
zLocalIpAddresses	A regular expression match to identify local IP address.
zMaxOIDPerRequest	Specify the number of OIDs Zenoss collects with a single query. The default is 40.
zPingInterfaceDescription	Find interfaces to ping by device description.
zPingInterfaceName	Find interfaces to ping by name.
zPingMonitorIgnore	Select true not to ping the device or false to ping the device.
zProdStateThreshold	Monitor a service that is higher than the production state listed. Possible values include 1000 (Production), 500 (Pre-Production), 400 (Test), 300 (Maintenance), and -1 (Decommissioned).
zRouteMapCollectOnlyIndirect	Set to true to collect only the indirect routes. Default is false.
zRouteMapCollectOnlyLocal	Set to true to collect only the local routes. Default is false.
zSnmpAuthPassword	Specify SNMP password, if applicable.
zSnmpAuthType	If using zSnmpAuthPassword, select either MD5 or SHA authentication protocol.
zSnmpCommunities	List of communities Zenoss tries to collect information for. The defaults are public and private. Enter more as needed.
zSnmpCommunity	The default community name on the monitored device.
zSnmpMonitorIgnore	Set whether or not Zenoss should monitor the device with SNMP. Defaults to false.
zSnmpPort	The SNMP communication port. Defaults to port 161.
zSnmpPrivPassword	Enter the security user's password.
zSnmpPrivType	Select either AES or DES encryption.
zSnmpSecurityName	enter the security user's name.
zSnmpTimeout	Length of time in seconds that Zenoss waits for a response from the remote SNMP agent. Defaults to 2.5.

zProperty	Description
zSnmpTries	Number of times Zenoss tries to connect via SNMP before reporting a failure.
zSnmpVer	The version of SNMP. Available options are 1, 2c, and 3. Defaults to 1.
zStatusConnectTimeout	Specifies the time in seconds for an IP service to respond before the service is marked down. The default is 15.
zSysedgeDiskMapIngoreNames	Not used.
zTelnetEnable	On Cisco routers, send the enable command to enable command collection. Default is false.
zTelnetEnableRegex	Match the enable prompt with the specified regular expression.
zTelnetLoginRegex	Match the login prompt with the specified regular expression.
zTelnetPasswordRegex	Match the password prompt with the specified regular expression.
zTelnetPromptTimeout	Specify the time in seconds to wait for the login prompt to display.
zTelnetSuccessRegexList	Match the command prompt with the specified regular expression.
zTelnetTermLength	Select true to enable telnet terminal length.
zWinEventLog	Specifies whether or not Zenoss collects the Windows event log. Default is false.
zWinEventLogMinSeverity	Collect all Windows event logs that match the specified severity. Enter a value between 1 and 5, where 1 is the most severe. The default is 2.
zWinPassword	Enter the Windows user's password.
zWinUser	Enter the user name of an account on the monitored Windows system.
zWmiMonitorIgnore	Set to true to ignore WMI monitoring and set to false to monitor WMI services.
zFileSystemMapIgnoreTypes	Do not use
zPythonClass	Do not use
zXmlRpcMonitorIgnore	Set to true to enable XML/RPC monitoring

Summary

As we see, Zenoss aggregates a large amount of information about our networks. In this chapter, we've learnt how to use classes, plug-ins, and modeling protocols to organize, collect, and display information about our devices. By using the device classes, we can define a hierarchical set of monitoring properties for groups of devices.

The classes allow us to set the collector plug-ins and define a common set of zProperties per device. Exceptions can be made on a per device basis. This is one of Zenoss's core data organization concepts. We can change a device's class or zProperties at any time and Zenoss will apply the changes the next time it models the device.

In Chapter 6, we will review status and performance monitors, and we will also monitor individual device components based on the device models we generated in this Chapter. We'll monitor TCI/IP services, processes, file systems, CPUs, and interfaces.

6
Status and Performance Monitors

Is the device available? How has the device performed over time? We answer these questions and more in our discussion about status and performance monitors. Status monitoring lets us know if the device is up or down, and performance monitoring graphs device performance over a time range.

In the previous chapters, we have built an inventory of the devices we wish to monitor and Zenoss is happily monitoring them. However, Zenoss makes its best guess about how we want to monitor our devices, which isn't always the way we want to monitor.

In this chapter, we learn how to tell Zenoss what and how we want to monitor. We'll start by reviewing the system-wide monitors we use to collect status and performance data. Then we'll monitor the interfaces, processes, services, file systems, and routes of a device. After we overview the performance graphs, we'll finish the chapter by customizing the threshold of a performance template.

Available Monitors

Zenoss provides one performance monitor and one status monitor by default. The monitors store information about how Zenoss collects monitoring information from the devices on the network. We can customize the existing monitors or create new monitors and apply them to devices or device classes.

To display the available status and performance monitors, select **Monitors** from the navigation panel.

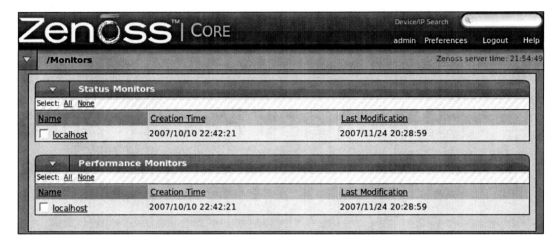

The tables provide the **Name**, the **Creation Time**, and the **Last Modification** time for each monitor as shown in the previous screenshot. We'll take a closer look at each one.

Status Monitors

Status monitors set the frequency at which Zenoss polls the devices for an up/down status. Zenoss allows us to configure how we perform ping tests. For example, we may configure a separate status monitor for our WAN sites than for our LAN sites. Click on the localhost status monitor to display the overview page. The **Overview** page shows the **Status Monitor Configuration** and **Devices** tables as shown in the following screenshot.

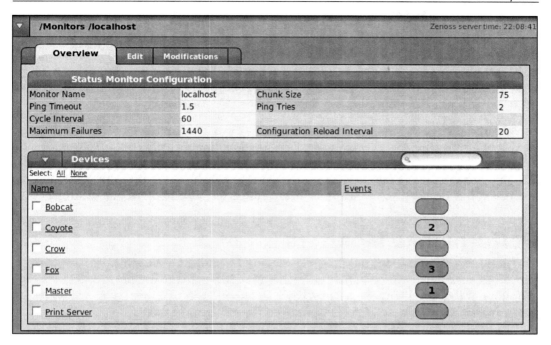

The **Status Monitor Configuration** provides a snapshot of the configuration as it exists. Our Zenoss installation currently uses this configuration to monitor the availability of all the devices, but we will add a new monitor soon. Let's review the available settings:

Property	Description
Monitor Name	A text description of the status monitor.
Ping Timeout	The time in seconds that zenping waits for a reply to the ping command. Default is 1.5.
Cycle Interval	The time in seconds for which Zenoss collects availability data. The default is 60 seconds.
Maximum Failures	If the device fails to respond to a ping for the specified number of consecutive tries, remove it. The default is 1440 (36 hours).
Chunk Size	Specifies a default chunk size of 75 bytes.
Ping Tries	The maximum number ping attempts per Cycle Interval. The default is 2.
Configuration Reload Interval	The time in minutes at which Zenoss reloads the configuration. The default is 20.

For our purposes, the most important values are **Ping Timeout**, **Cycle Interval**, and **Ping Tries**. Let's step through an example using the default values. Zenoss pings the device each minute. If the device fails to respond to the first ping within 1.5 seconds, a second ping is sent. If the device fails to acknowledge the second ping within 1.5 seconds, Zenoss marks the device as down (red) and generates an event. If the device returns the ping, Zenoss marks the device status as up (green).

If we make changes to the localhost status monitor, we affect the way Zenoss monitors all the devices. For example, if we decide that we only need to check for available devices once every five minutes, we could change the Cycle Interval to 300. If we have a device or class of devices we want to monitor at a different interval, such as WAN devices, we create a different status monitor to store our settings.

Performance Monitors

The performance monitors tell Zenoss how often to collect data about the services, processes, and hardware attached to the devices. We manage the performance monitors in the same way we manage the status monitors. To display the default performance monitors, select Monitors from the navigation menu.

Click on the localhost performance monitor to display the monitor's **Overview** page. The **Overview** page shows the **Performance Collector Configuration** table and the **Devices** table (refer to following screenshot).

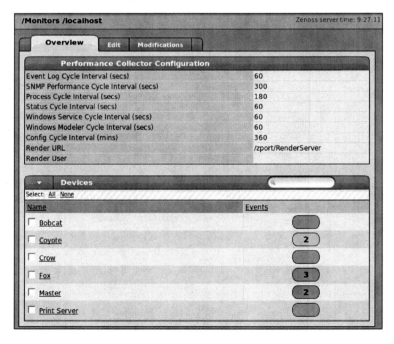

The **Performance Collector Configuration** table displays the current configuration settings, and the **Devices** table shows a list of all the devices using the localhost performance monitor. Since localhost is the default, our entire device inventory displays in the **Devices** list.

Let's review the performance collector settings.

Property	Description
Event Log Cycle Interval	The time in seconds for which zenwin collects Windows event logs. The default is **60**.
SNMP Performance Cycle Interval	The time in seconds for which zenperfsnmp collects SNMP performance data. The default is **300**.
Process Cycle Interval	The time in seconds for which zenprocess collects process performance data. The default is **180**.
Status Cycle Interval	The time in seconds for which zenstatus collects data about TCP services . The default is **60**.
Windows Service Cycle Interval	The time in seconds for which zenwin collects performance data about Windows services. The default is **60**.
Windows Modeler Cycle Interval	The time in seconds for which zenwinmodeler collects performance data. The default is **60**.
Config Cycle Interval	The time in minutes that Zenoss reloads the monitor configuration.
Render URL	Used for inter-daemon communication (XML/RPC) for graphing information. The default is **/zport/RenderServer**.
Render User	The user name required to connect to a remote collector plugin. Default is blank.

To make changes to the localhost performance monitor, click the **Edit** tab. Any changes we make here affects all the devices assigned to this performance monitor.

The Edit page includes two fields that do not display on the **Overview** page: Render Password and Default RRD Create Command. The **Render User** and the **Render Password** values allow the Zenoss system to authenticate to a remote performance collector. We only need to specify a user name and password if our Zenoss system needs to communicate directly with a remote performance collector.

The Default RRD Create Command field contains syntax for the RRDTool to use to build graphs. The default configuration should be fine, but for more information about RRDTool visit `http://oss.oetiker.ch/rrdtool/`.

Add A New Monitor

We use the same process to add a status monitor as we do to add a performance monitor; therefore, we'll demonstrate the process by adding an example status monitor.

In our example, we add a new monitor named "Workstation.":

1. Select Monitors from the navigation menu.
2. From the Status Monitors table menu, select Add Monitor.
3. Enter a descriptive name (Eg.: Workstation) in the Add Monitor dialog box.
4. Click OK to confirm the add.

The new monitor displays in the Status Monitor list, but it has the same settings as the localhost status monitor. Click on the new Workstation monitor name to display the Overview page. Notice that the Workstation status monitor does not have any devices attached to it.

Before we assign the new monitor to any devices, let's configure it. Click the Edit tab. We change the Cycle Interval to 0 so that any devices assigned to the monitor will not be pinged. However, the devices will still be modeled.

Attach A Monitor To Devices

After we add and configure the monitor, we need to attach it to a device. This example uses our new status monitor to demonstrate the steps, but we would apply the same steps to performance monitors.

We either assign the monitor to an individual device or to a device class, so that all the devices in the class inherit the monitor.

To change the monitor for a group of individual devices:

1. Select **Device List** from the navigation menu.
2. Select the target devices.
3. From the page menu, select **Set Status Monitor**.
4. Choose **Workstation** from the **Status Monitor** selection box (refer to the following screenshot).
5. Click **OK** to confirm the change.

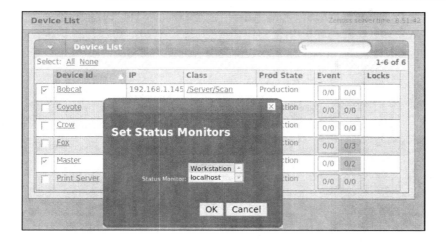

To change the status monitor for an entire device class:

1. Select Devices from the navigation menu to display the list of classes.
2. Click the Workstation class name that we created in Chapter 5 from the Sub-Devices table.
3. From the page menu, select **Edit > Set Status Monitors**.
4. Select **Workstation** from the **Status Monitor** selection box (refer to the following screenshot).
5. Click **OK** to confirm the change.

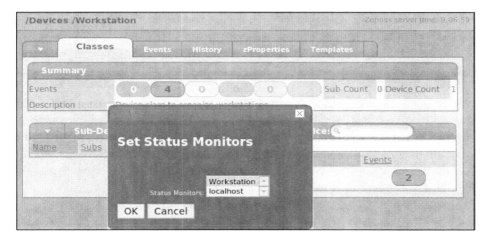

Next, we verify that our devices reflect the new status monitors. We could look at the Edit tab for each device to see if the Workstation status monitor is set for the device, but , we'll continue working from the Monitors Overview page.

Select **Monitors** from the navigation menu. Then follow the Workstation link to display the **Overview** page. The **Devices** list shows all the devices using the Workstation status monitor.

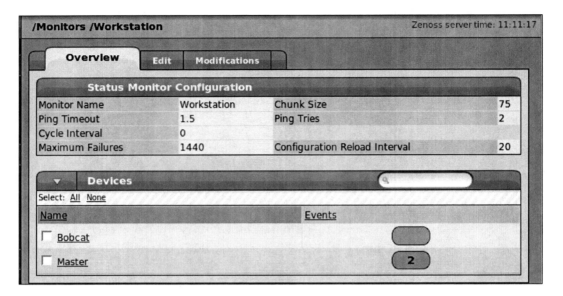

Component Status

Now that we know a bit about how Zenoss collects status and performance information, we turn our attention to monitoring the status of the components. We manage the individual components of a device from the OS tab.

OS Tab

When we select a device from the Device List, the OS tab becomes available. The components listed on the OS tab depend upon the device, the modeling protocol (for example, SNMP, SSH, port scan) and the collector plug-ins used for the device; therefore not all the devices will have the same components listed. We'll cover each of the following components in turn: Interfaces, OS Process, IP Services, Win Services, File Systems, and Routes.

Interfaces

As part of the modeling process, Zenoss discovers the interfaces running on the device and automatically begins monitoring them. The following screenshot shows the discovered interfaces on our example server, Fox, along with various bits of configuration information, including the interface **Name**, **IP Address**, **Network**, **MAC** address, operational status, administrative status, and whether or not the device configuration is locked. We covered locks in Chapter 5. The operational status is represented by the "**O**" column heading, while the "**A**" column represents the administrative status.

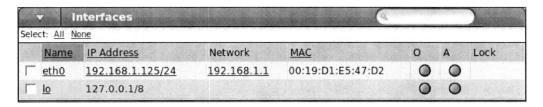

Since Fox is a Linux server, we will check Zenoss' work by logging in and running the following command to see if the interface information matches up:

```
ifconfig -a
```

Windows users can run the following command to see a list of all the interfaces:

```
ipconfig /all
```

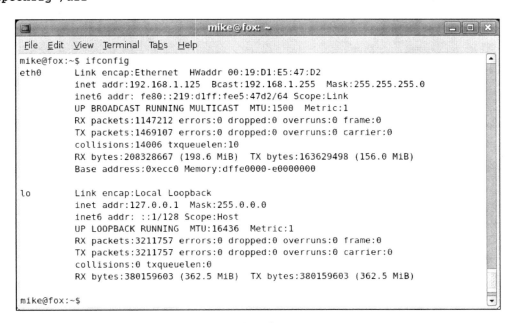

As we see, the list of interfaces in Zenoss matches the interfaces found on the device. However, just because Zenoss discovers the interface doesn't mean we need to monitor it. For example, we may decide we don't really need to monitor the loopback adapter.

The loopback adapter (lo) provides an interface for network traffic that only takes place on the local machine, and it always has an IP address of 127.0.0.1. We do not want to delete the loopback adapter from our machine, as that would cause problems, but we can delete the monitor from Zenoss without any problems.

To delete the "lo" interface from the list, select it and choose **Delete IpInterfaces** from the Interfaces table menu.

We can also add interfaces to Zenoss. To add the "lo" interface, select **Add IpInterfaces** from the Interfaces table menu. Enter "lo" in the ID field of the **Add IpInterface** dialog box. After we add the interface name, Zenoss displays the Interface Status page (refer to the following screenshot).

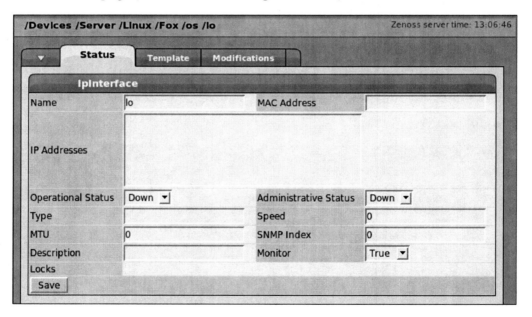

If we specify the **Name, IP Address**, and a **Monitor** status equal to **True**, all other values will be detected the next time Zenoss models the device. Actually, in case of our example, Zenoss would have added the loopback adapter back to the Interfaces list automatically the next time it modeled the device. If we do not want to monitor an interface, set the **Monitor** status to false. Save the changes and navigate back to the OS page.

OS Processes

Zenoss keeps tabs on almost any process we want to monitor. Zenoss won't be able to gather reliable statistics for short-lived processes which up at irregular intervals. On the server, each running application is represented by a process. From the navigation menu, select Processes. The Classes tab displays a Sub-Folders and Processes table.

To add a process:

1. Select Add Process from the Processes table menu.
2. Enter the name of the process (for example mysql) in the ID field of the Add OSProcess dialog box.
3. Click OK to create the process monitor.

Now, add a second process name, such as snmp.exe.

The **Processes** table lists the monitored processes by **Name** along with the regular expression (**Regex**) Zenoss uses to identify the process on the device. The **Monitor** column tells us whether or not the process is being monitored, and the **Count** column indicates the number of monitored instances of each process (refer to the following screenshot).

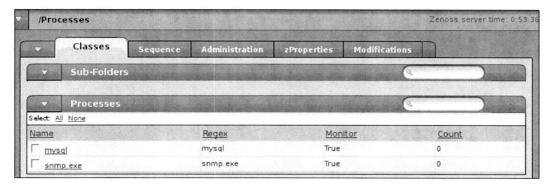

As we see, Zenoss populates the Regex value based on the value we entered when we added the process. If we want to specify a Python-based regular expression, for our process:

1. Click on the mysql process to display the Status page.
2. Click on the Edit tab.
3. Enter .*mysql.* in the Regex field.
4. Click Save.

We use the Sub-Folders to create organizers for our processes. Since Zenoss can monitor Windows and Linux processes, we'll organize our process monitors by operating system.

To add a new Sub-Folder to the Processes page:

1. Select Add New Organizer from the Sub-Folders table menu.
2. Enter the name of the organizer (for example, Windows) in the ID field of the Add Organizer dialog box.
3. Click OK to create the new organizer.
4. For the sake of completeness, add a second organizer for Linux.

Let's finish organizing our processes by moving the Linux processes to the Linux folder and the Windows processes to the Windows folder.

To move a process to a folder:

1. Select the process from the Processes table.
2. Select Move Processes from the table menu.
3. Select the folder name from the drop-down list in the Move Processes dialog box.
4. Click Move to assign the process to an organizer.

The next time Zenoss models the devices, it automatically detects and adds the new processes to the device's monitored components. Let's take a look at the OS tab for our test server, Fox.

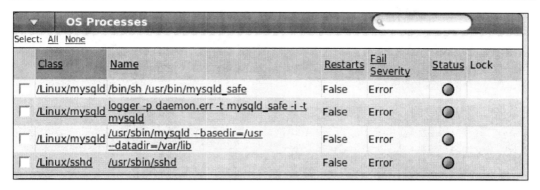

From the previous screenshot, we see that Zenoss detected and added several instances of the `mysqld` process and one `sshd` process. The **OS Processes** table displays the service **Class**, **Name**, alert status for **Restarts**, **Fail Severity**, **Status**, and configuration **Locks**.

If we follow the service class link, Zenoss displays the class properties. In addition to the current configuration, we see a Process Instances table that lists each monitored instance of the process and its status. The following screenshot shows the sshd service class.

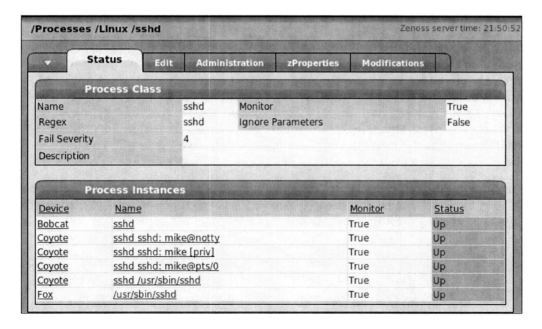

If we navigate back to the device's OS tab, we can click on a process's class name from the OS Processes table to display a settings screen. The available settings are intuitive. We have a **Status**, a link to the **Process Class**, the **Name** of the process, the **Monitor** status, **Alert On Restart** status, and the **Fail Severity** (refer to the following screenshot).

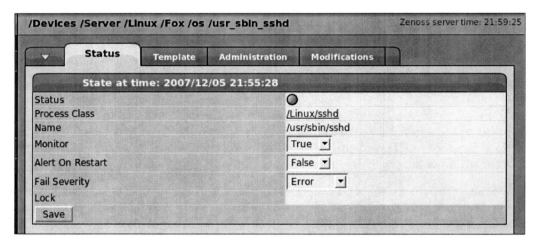

Services

Unlike processes, Zenoss provides a list of services available to monitor, on the devices. Services start automatically when the operating system boots up and without the need for user control. Windows services (for example, eventlog) and Unix daemons (for example, smtp) are examples of services. To view the list of services, select Services from the navigation menu. The Services are organized by folders for IpService and WinService, and each provides a count of the number of included services; the IpService contains a list of Linux-based services while the WinService organizer contains a list of Windows-based services.

By clicking on the folder name, we navigate the list of services and sub-folders. For example, the IpService folder contains further divisions for privileged and registered ports. The Privileged folder contains those ports up to 1024.

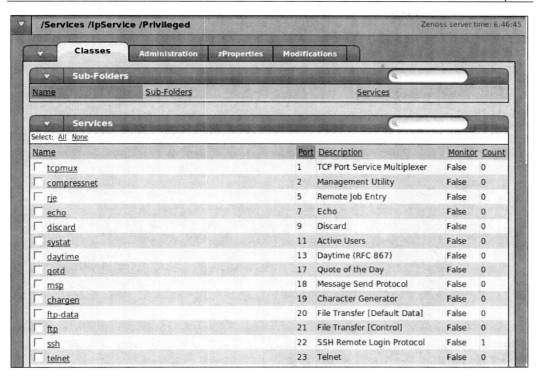

The **Services** table displays several columns of information for each service name, including **Port, Description, Monitor** status, and a service **Count**. The **Monitor** status indicates whether the service class is monitored by default or not. We can automatically monitor services as Zenoss discovers them, by setting the monitor status to true, or we can enable monitoring for individual devices.

Click on the ssh service name to display the ssh service class **Status** page (refer to the following screenshot). This page has a similar format as the process class status page.

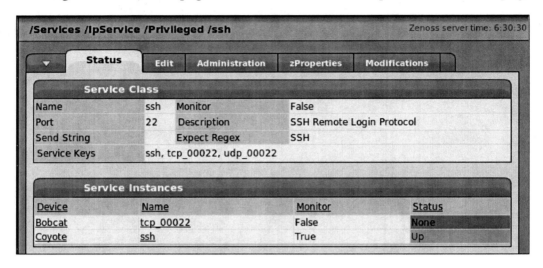

The **Service Class** table lists the current configuration as defined on the **Edit** tab and **zProperties** tab. The **Service Instances** table lists all the occurrences of the service by **Device** along with the **Monitor** status and operational **Status**.

We can set the failure severity and monitor status on the **zProperties** tab. Select the **Edit** tab to modify additional service properties, including the name, description, and port. We can also control what Zenoss checks when monitoring the service by specifying a Send String value, and then defining the expected response in the Expect Regex field.

Any change we make here will apply to all instances of the service, and the next time Zenoss models the devices, the device model updates automatically.

IP Services

Sometimes, we won't want to monitor all instances of a service, and in those cases, we can add IP Services from the device's OS tab. In this example, we'll monitor the syslog service for the device, Fox. From the OS tab, we have two ways to add a service.

If Zenoss is currently monitoring any service, we see an IP Services table with a list of services. In this case, we can choose Add IpService from the table menu.

If we don't see the IP Services menu, then we can use the page menu and select **Add > IpService**:

1. When the **Add IpService** dialog displays begin typing the name of the service (for example, **sysl**) and notice the list of services filters as we type.
2. Select the service from the list (for example, **syslog**).
3. Select the protocol of the service you want to monitor (E.g: tcp or udp)
3. Click **OK** to add the new service.

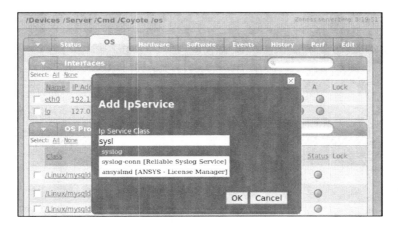

Zenoss displays a service **Status** page after we add the service. This screen is a remix of the service class properties we reviewed in the previous section. If we need to, we can change settings, such as the **Protocol** and the **Port** number. In order to get Zenoss to monitor the syslog service on the device, we need to set the **Monitor** status to **True** (refer to the following screenshot).

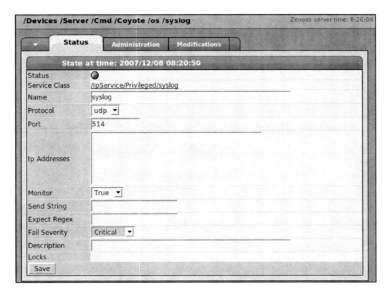

After we save the configuration, the status indicator turns from gray to green, indicating that the service is monitored and available.

Now, when we navigate back to the OS tab for the device, we see the syslog service in the **IP Services** table. By default, the table displays the monitored services; however, if we want to see a list of the unmonitored services for the device, uncheck the **Monitored** checkbox in the **IP Services** table heading (refer to the following screenshot).

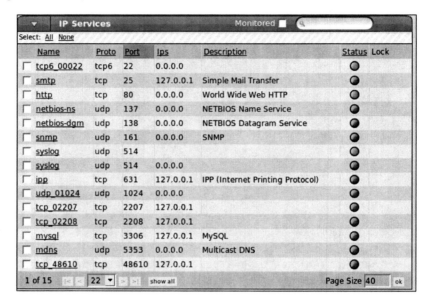

To enable monitoring for any service in this list, click on the Service name to edit the properties and set the Monitor status to true.

Win Services

In order to monitor Windows services, WMI must be installed on the Windows machines. For help in installing WMI, refer to Chapter 3. To demonstrate the Win Services, let's build a software inventory for our test device Master by monitoring the AppMgmt service:

1. From the page menu, select **Add > Add WinService**.

2. In the **Win Service Class** field, begin typing the name of the service (for example, app as shown in the following screenshot) to filter the list.

3. Select the service name (for example, **AppMgmt**).

4. Click **OK** to add the WinService.

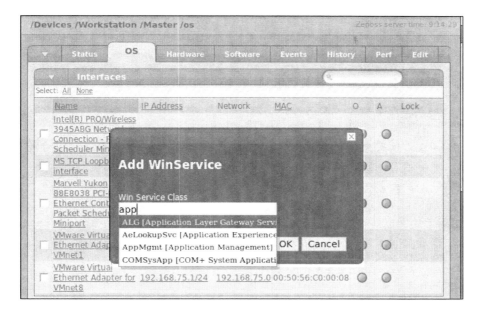

After we add the service, we need to set the Monitor status to true and save the change, just like we did with the IP Services.

In addition to monitoring the availability of the Windows Applications Management service, Zenoss will populate the **Software** tab with a list of all the installed software when the device is modeled (refer to the following screenshot).

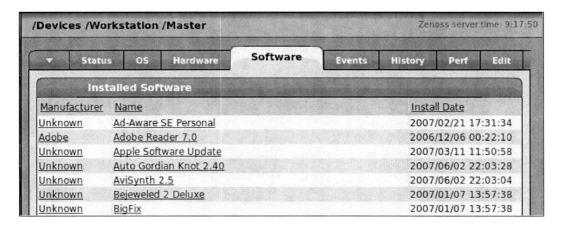

File Systems

Zenoss models the file system hierarchy and reports the volume, capacity in **Total bytes, Used bytes, Free bytes, Percent Utilization,** and whether or not the file system configuration is locked (refer to the following screenshot). If we add a new **Mount** point, such as an extra drive, Zenoss automatically detects and adds the new file system when it models the device.

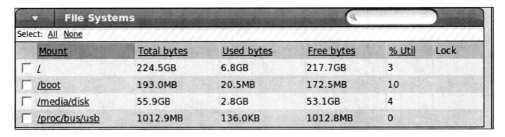

We can also manually add a new file system from the OS tab:

1. From the File Systems table menu, select Add File System.

2. In the ID field of the Add File System Dialog, enter the mount point for the file system (E.g: /media/disk).

3. Click OK to add the new file system.

Zenoss displays the **Status** page of the of the new **File System** with several properties. The only values we need to verify are the **Mount Point** and the **Monitor** status. After we verify the **Mount Point** and set the **Monitor** status to **True** as shown in the following screenshot, we will **Save** our changes.

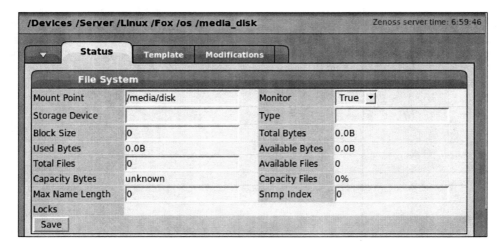

When we navigate back to the OS tab, notice that the new file system for /media/ disk does not have the total bytes, free bytes, used bytes, and utilization calculated. After Zenoss models the device, the file system details fill in.

Routes

For each device, Zenoss discovers the routing table and displays the following information in the **Routes** table of the OS tab: **Destination, NextHop, Interface, Protocol, Type,** and configuration **Locks** (as shown in the following screenshot). If the Destination or **NextHop** values correspond to a discovered network, then we can click on the route to display the network properties. We have added and configured networks in Chapter 4. Likewise, if we click on the interface name, we load the interface status page from the Interfaces table on the OS tab.

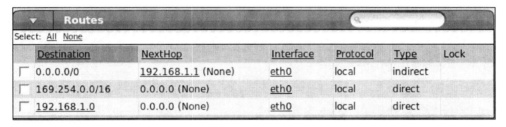

Similar to the interfaces, we can easily verify whether Zenoss is providing us with accurate information or not. If we log on to Fox, we can issue the following command to see a list of routes:

```
routes -n
```

On a Windows server, we can use the following command:

```
route print
```

```
mike@fox:~$ route -n
Kernel IP routing table
Destination     Gateway         Genmask         Flags Metric Ref    Use Iface
192.168.1.0     0.0.0.0         255.255.255.0   U     0      0        0 eth0
169.254.0.0     0.0.0.0         255.255.0.0     U     1000   0        0 eth0
0.0.0.0         192.168.1.1     0.0.0.0         UG    0      0        0 eth0
mike@fox:~$
```

Although Zenoss automatically adds new routes that it discovers when it models the device, we can add a new route manually:

1. From the Routes table menu, select Add IpRouteEntry.
2. The AddIpRouteEntry dialog box prompts for several values:
   ° Destination
   ° Next Hop
   ° Interface
   ° Protocol
   ° Type
3. Enter at least the destination address.
4. Click OK to add the route.

The next time Zenoss models the device, it will fill in any route details you left blank while adding the new route.

Performance Graphs

Zenoss creates time series graphs using RRDTool for the performance monitors we discussed earlier in the chapter. "Time series" implies that we continuously measure data at regular intervals. We find graphs in two locations. The device's **Perf** tab contains **load**, cpu, and memory utilization graphs. From the **OS** tab, we can view graphs for the interfaces, OS processes, and file systems.

All graphs on a page share display settings. Each group of graphs can be viewed on an **Hourly**, daily, weekly, monthly, or yearly **Range**. The default **Range** is **Hourly** (see the following screenshot). Each group of graphs has a **Reset** button that restores all the graphs on a page to the default view. The **Link graphs** check box allows all the graphs on the page to stay in synchronisation as we navigate through the time line of a single graph.

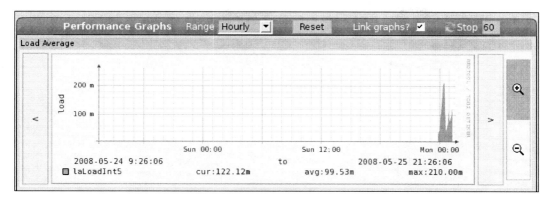

Each graph also has its own set of controls. On either side of the graph, we have time line navigation controls. The "<" navigates backward through the date range while the ">" navigates forward. The magnifying glasses allow us to zoom in and out on the graph. To zoom in, click the "+", and then move the cursor over the graph. When the cursor turns to a cross hairs, click the mouse button to zoom in. The same process applies to zoom out, except that we select the "-" magnifying glass.

The layout of each graph also follows a common format. The time measurement plots on the x axis and the data point being measured plots on the y-axis. Beneath the x-axis, the graph identifies the visible time range.

At the bottom of the graph, we see the color-coded data points represented on the graph. Each data point displays current, average, and maximum measurements for the visible time range.

On the device's **Perf** tab, Zenoss displays the following default graphs:

- Load Average
- Load Average 5 Min
- CPU Utilization
- CPU Idle
- Free Swap
- Free Memory

Of the graphs listed on the **Perf** tab, only the CPU Idle graph establishes an event generating threshold. If idle CPU percentage drops below 2%, Zenoss generates a warning event.

Additional performance graphs are available from the OS tab for:

- Interfaces
  - ○ Throughput
  - ○ Packets
  - ○ Errors
- OS Processes
  - ○ CPU Utilization
  - ○ Memory
  - ○ Process Count
- File Systems
  - ○ Utilization

To view the graphs for an individual interface, process, or file system, click the name from the applicable table to view the properties. The graphs display on the second half of the page. For example, if we want to see the utilization graph for the root file system on Fox, we first navigate to the OS tab for Fox. Then we click on the "/" name from the File Systems table to display the status page. Then we can scroll down the page to view the Utilization graph.

Default thresholds are established for interfaces and file systems. When the interface reaches at least 75% utilization or when a file system usage exceeds 90%, Zenoss generates a warning event.

In order to change or add our graphs, including thresholds, we modify the device's performance template.

Performance Templates

Performance templates tell Zenoss what data sources to collect and how to graph the data. They use that data to establish monitoring thresholds, which we can in turn use to generate events. We apply template properties to the devices class or to the individual device. In Zenoss terminology, the process of applying a template to a device or a class is called binding.

To view the templates that are bound to a device class, navigate to the class (for example, /Server/Linux) and click the **Templates** tab (shown in the following screenshot).

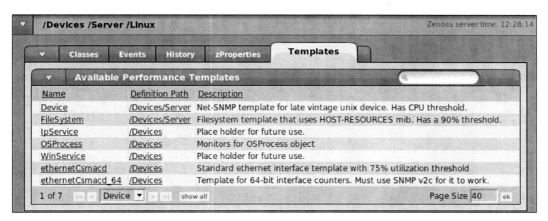

Let's compare the template bindings for the /Server/Linux device class with that of the device Fox, a member of the /Server/Linux group. Navigate to the Status Overview page for Fox, and from the page menu, select **More > Templates** (refer to the following screenshot).

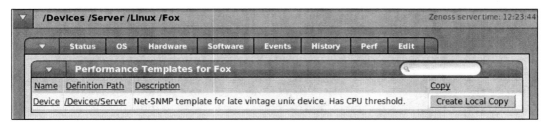

All of the templates applied to the class level apply to Fox and when Zenoss creates the graphs, it searches the device class hierarchy and matches the graph to the monitored component. This way, if we monitor a file system, Zenoss automatically creates a performance graph for the file system. Since the Device template is bound to Fox at the device level, Zenoss applies those template settings and ignores the template settings defined for the Device template bound to the device class.

Click on the Device name from the device class templates page to display the template properties. In addition to the name and description, we see the tables for Data Sources, Thresholds, and Graph Definitions.

The Device performance template we are viewing defines the graphs we previously reviewed on the Perf tab.

Data Sources

The **Data Sources** table lists the **Name, Source, Source Type,** and **Enabled** status for each data source (see the following screenshot). The **Source** lists the individual OID that Zenoss polls to collect the performance data. For example, to get system up time, Zenoss polls the 1.3.6.1.2.1.25.1.1.0 OID.

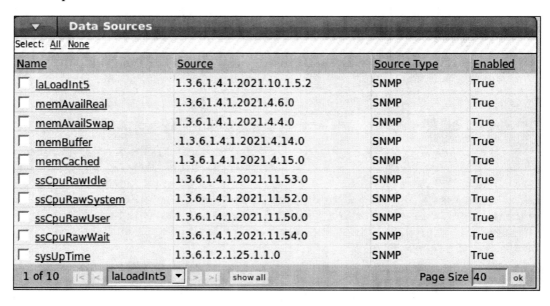

Name	Source	Source Type	Enabled
laLoadInt5	1.3.6.1.4.1.2021.10.1.5.2	SNMP	True
memAvailReal	1.3.6.1.4.1.2021.4.6.0	SNMP	True
memAvailSwap	1.3.6.1.4.1.2021.4.4.0	SNMP	True
memBuffer	.1.3.6.1.4.1.2021.4.14.0	SNMP	True
memCached	.1.3.6.1.4.1.2021.4.15.0	SNMP	True
ssCpuRawIdle	1.3.6.1.4.1.2021.11.53.0	SNMP	True
ssCpuRawSystem	1.3.6.1.4.1.2021.11.52.0	SNMP	True
ssCpuRawUser	1.3.6.1.4.1.2021.11.50.0	SNMP	True
ssCpuRawWait	1.3.6.1.4.1.2021.11.54.0	SNMP	True
sysUpTime	1.3.6.1.2.1.25.1.1.0	SNMP	True

1 of 10   laLoadInt5   show all   Page Size 40   ok

The **Source Type** is either **SNMP** or command by default. Additional source types, such as JMX are available through ZenPacks. Fox uses SNMP to monitor the OID, but the command source type collects data by running shell commands. For comparison, let's look at the **Data Sources** table for Coyote, a device monitored via SSH. The sources look quite different. Instead of OID values, we see the Zenoss Plug-ins we installed in Chapter 5, as shown in the following screenshot.

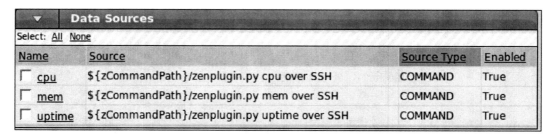

Name	Source	Source Type	Enabled
cpu	${zCommandPath}/zenplugin.py cpu over SSH	COMMAND	True
mem	${zCommandPath}/zenplugin.py mem over SSH	COMMAND	True
uptime	${zCommandPath}/zenplugin.py uptime over SSH	COMMAND	True

To configure the data source and edit the data points, click on the name from the table. SNMP data sources have exactly one data point, while each command data source may have more than one data point.

Thresholds

The performance template page lists any established thresholds by **Name**, **Type**, **Data Source**, **Severity**, and **Enabled** status, as shown in the following screenshot. The only threshold type Zenoss includes by default is **MinMaxThreshold**, which allows us to monitor the minimum or maximum values of a data source. We apply the threshold against one of the data sources defined in the **Data Sources** table.

▼	Thresholds			
Select: <u>All</u> <u>None</u>				
Name	Type	Data Sources	Severity	Enabled
☐ <u>CPU Utilization</u>	MinMaxThreshold	ssCpuRawIdle_ssCpuRawIdle	Warning	True

To configure the **CPU Utilization** threshold in our example, click on the name. From the Min/Max Threshold configuration page, we should recognize the settings from the example we used when talking about the CPU Idle performance graph:

- Data Points = ssCpuRawIdle_ssCpuRawIdle
- Min Value = 2
- Severity = warning
- Escalate = 5

This means if the Idle CPU usage falls below 2%, Zenoss generates a warning event and if the usage remains below 2% for five consecutive monitoring periods, Zenoss escalates the event to an error severity.

Graph Definitions

The final table on the performance templates page is **Graph Definitions** which lists the graphs to display according to **Sequence, Name, Graph Points, Units, Height,** and **Width,** as shown in the following screenshot. The **Graph Points** correspond to the data points. The units specify the unit of measure displayed on the y-axis of the graph. The default **Height** and **Width** values are **100** and **500** pixels, respectively.

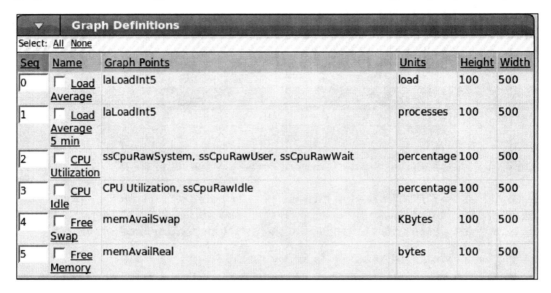

Seq	Name	Graph Points	Units	Height	Width
0	☐ Load Average	laLoadInt5	load	100	500
1	☐ Load Average 5 min	laLoadInt5	processes	100	500
2	☐ CPU Utilization	ssCpuRawSystem, ssCpuRawUser, ssCpuRawWait	percentage	100	500
3	☐ CPU Idle	CPU Utilization, ssCpuRawIdle	percentage	100	500
4	☐ Free Swap	memAvailSwap	KBytes	100	500
5	☐ Free Memory	memAvailReal	bytes	100	500

To configure a graph, click on its name. If our data graphs exponentially, we can show a logarithmic y-axis by setting the Log value to true. To graph data that is measured in multiples of 1024, set Base 1024 to true. We can change the way the values get displayed on the y-axis by specifying a Min or Max Y value.

Reorder The Graphs on The Perf Tab

The Seq field on the Graph Definitions table identifies the order in which the graphs are displayed when viewing the Perf tab. To change the order of the graphs:

1. Type the preferred sequence next to each graph.
2. From the Graph Definitions table menu, select Re-sequence Graphs.

Now, when we view the Perf tab for the device, the graphs get displayed in our preferred order.

If we want to delete a graph entirely, select the graph name, and choose Delete Graph from the Graph Definitions table menu.

Customize A Threshold

Instead of editing the default templates and changing the original settings, we can create a copy of the template to edit. Let's tweak our CPU Utilization threshold for Fox.

From the Templates page for Fox, click the Create Local Copy button for the Device template. The button name now says **Remove Local Copy** and Zenoss displays a status message confirming the action (see following screenshot).

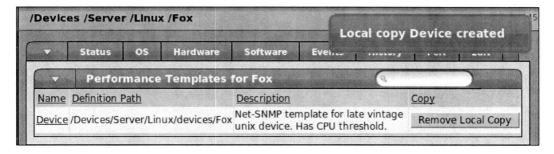

1. Edit the Device template by clicking on its name.
2. Edit the CPU Utilization threshold.
3. Change the Name to Sensitive CPU Utilization.
4. Change the Min Value to 5.
5. Change the Escalate Count to 3.
6. Save the changes.

Now, Zenoss generates a warning event if the idle CPU percentage for Fox falls below 5%, and if the idle CPU percentage remains below 5% for three consecutive polling periods, Zenoss escalates the event severity to error.

Of course, we can change any value on our template to meet our monitoring needs, including Data Sources and Graph Definitions. For an example of adding a new performance template with new Data Sources and Graph Definitions, see the HttpMonitor ZenPack section in Chapter 10.

Summary

In this chapter, we learnt how Zenoss monitors our devices and their processes, services, and components. Not only do we know if our devices are available, but we can graph key performance metrics over time too. The status and performance monitoring concepts we discussed in this chapter enable us to customize our Zenoss monitoring environment so that we track and report only the information we want to see.

By defining our monitoring properties, we give Zenoss a set of rules to apply to the devices on our network. When Zenoss finds a device that is not operating within the bounds of our expected rules, it generates an event. In the next chapter, we learn how to process events in Zenoss.

7
Event Management

When problems occur on our networks, we want to know about them. Zenoss notifies us of the problems by generating events when one of our devices becomes unavailable or crosses a performance threshold.

In Zenoss, we have several ways to view and manipulate events for our devices. We'll start off by setting Zenoss to monitor Unix syslogs and Windows event logs. Then we'll tour the Event Console, event classes, and the Event Manager, and we'll finish the chapter by building custom event rules.

The Event Console helps us identify and work with active events. We use event classes to define our event processing rules via event class keys, Python scripts, and TALES expressions. The Event Manager enables us to change the way in which Zenoss stores and displays events.

Monitor Syslog Messages

In Zenoss, we have the capability to monitor syslog messages from Unix-based hosts on the network. Zenoss uses the zensyslog daemon to turn incoming syslog messages into events from any host on the network, even if the host is not in the Zenoss device inventory.

Before we configure our servers to send syslog messages to Zenoss, we need to determine the facility and priority we want to monitor. The available facilities include auth, authpriv, cron, daemon, ftp, kern, lpr, mail, news, syslog, user, and uucp. The facility specifies the subsystem we want to monitor. For example, we specify the lpr facility to monitor print activity.

We specify one of the following priorities, listed from the lowest to the highest severity: debug, info, notice, warning, err, crit, alert, and emerg. Choose the minimum priority to log. For example, choose warning to monitor logs with a priority of warning, err, crit alert and emerg.

In our `syslog.conf` file, we separate the facility and the priority by a period, as the example shows. Let's set up the sample Linux server. Coyote to send its syslog messages to Zenoss:

1. On Coyote, edit `/etc/syslog.conf` as root (refer to the following screenshot).

2. Add the following line where `192.168.1.125` is the IP address or the host name of the Zenoss server:

   `mail.debug @192.168.1.125`

3. Restart the syslog service as root:

   `/etc/init.d/sysklogd restart`

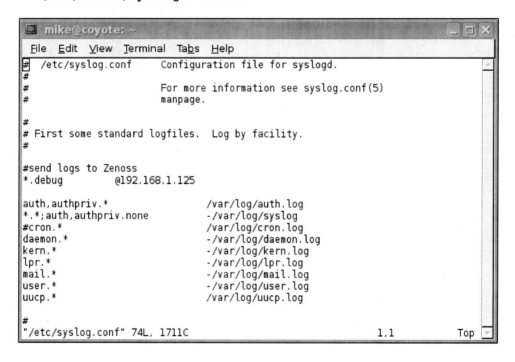

Note the `mail.debug` syntax in the syslog example. This sends all syslog facilities with a minimum priority of debug to the Zenoss. Based on our needs and the capabilities of `syslog.conf`, we can fine-tune our rules as needed. For more information about `syslog.conf`, see the documentation by running the command:

```
man syslog.conf
```

Of course, Unix-based servers are not the only devices that have remote syslog capabilities. Many routers provide remote logging features. We'll overview the steps needed for a Cisco router. For other devices, consult the documentation.

Collect Cisco Router Syslogs

To forward the Cisco router's syslogs to Zenoss, we need to know the Zenoss host, the minimum log priority to collect, and the facility. The following priorities are available: Emergency, alert, critical, error, warning, notice, informational, and debug. The available facilities include local0 through local7 and the default facility is local7.

To forward syslog messages from a Cisco IOS router to Zenoss, log onto the router and follow these steps using privileged EXEC mode:

1. Enter the configuration mode with the command:

   ```
   configure terminal
   ```

2. Specify the Zenoss server by IP address or host name with the command:

   ```
   logging 192.168.1.125
   ```

3. Set the syslog priority:

   ```
   logging trap warning
   ```

4. Set the syslog facility:

   ```
   logging facility local7
   ```

5. Quit the configuration mode:

   ```
   end
   ```

6. Verify the logging information:

   ```
   show logging
   ```

After we configure the device to send its logs to Zenoss, we need to configure the Zenoss system to monitor the syslogs:

1. Log in to Zenoss and open the OS tab for the device we configured for remote syslog logging.

2. From the IP Services table menu, select **Add IP Service**.

3. In the **Add IpService** dialog box, enter "**syslog**"(refer to the following screenshot).

4. Click **OK** to open the syslog Status page.

5. Change the Monitor status to True.

6. Click **Save** to begin monitoring the syslog service for the device.

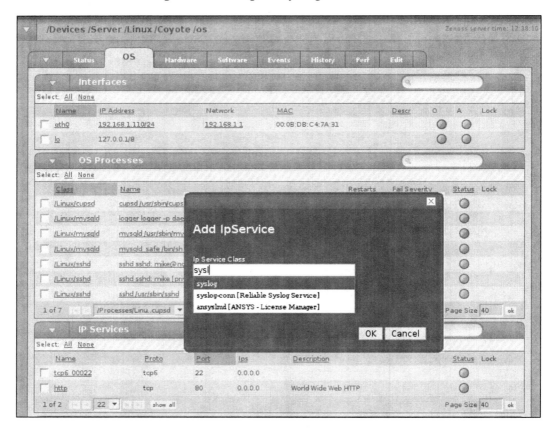

Zenoss is now monitoring the syslogs for a single device. If we want to monitor the syslog services on all devices, we enable monitoring at the syslog service class level as we discussed in Chapter 6.

Test Syslog Configuration with Logger

We can test our remote syslog configuration by using the command line tool "logger" to send a test syslog message of a specified facility and priority. To test, run the following commands from the Linux devices that are logging their messages to Zenoss:

```
logger -p cron.warn "This is a test"
logger -p mail.error "This is another test"
```

The logger command syntax is straightforward. The -p option specifies the facility and the priority which we followed with a message in quotes. Based on our earlier Linux syslog example where we directed all the mail subsystem messages with at least a priority of debug to Zenoss, the first command will not display in the Zenoss Event Console, but the second command will.

To double check, click on the Event Console and verify that the syslog messages are being logged correctly. By the end of this chapter, we'll know how to process the unknown event in the Event Console.

Monitor Windows Event Logs

In the Server Setup section of Chapter 3, we discussed setting up Windows Management Instrument ion (WMI). If WMI is not yet installed, take a few moments to review the instructions in Chapter 3.

Unlike syslog, which logs messages directly to a remote host, Zenoss has to connect to the Windows server to monitor the system's Event Log. We'll monitor the device Master, our sample Windows system:

1. Log in to Zenoss and open the OS tab for the device Master.
2. From the Win Services table menu, select Add WinServices.
3. In the Add WinServices dialog box, enter "Event Log.".
4. Click OK to open the Event Log Status page.
5. Change the monitor status to True.
6. Click Save.

Next, we need to configure the following device zProperties to connect to the Windows machine and monitor the event logs. From the device's Status page, select **More > zProperties** and enter the following configuration:

1. Set **zWinEventlog** to **True**.

2. Set **zWinPassword** to the password of the **zWinUser**.

3. Set **zWinUser** to a user who has administrative access to the Windows server.

4. For a domain user, specify `DOMAIN\user`.

5. For a local user, specify `.\user`.

6. Set **zWmiMonitorignore** to **False**.

zWinEventlog	True ▼	boolean	/Workstation/devices/Master
zWinEventlogMinSeverity	2	int	/
zWinPassword	******	string	/Workstation/devices/Master
zWinUser	Mike	string	/Workstation/devices/Master
zWmiMonitorignore	False ▼	boolean	/Workstation/devices/Master

By default, Zenoss collects the Windows events with a minimum severity of warning. But we can change that by specifying a value in the zWinEventlogMinSeverity. The following table shows the available event log severities:

Event Log Severity	Description
1	Error
2	Warning
4	Informational
8	Security Audit Success
16	Security Audit Failure

Test Event Log Configuration with Eventcreate

Windows provides a tool called `eventcreate.exe` that we can use to generate system events and test our Event Log setup. To test, run the following commands from a Windows device where Zenoss is monitoring the Event Log:

```
eventcreate /t error /l system /id 500 /d "test message"
eventcreate /t error /id 501 /d "another test message"
eventcreate /?
```

Let's look at the command syntax. We use the /t option to specify the severity, /l to specify either application or system message, /id to create an event id, and /d to include a message. The first command creates an system error message with an ID of 500 while the second command creates an application error message with an ID of 501. The third command displays the eventcreate.exe help page.

Event Console

From the Event Console, we see a single view of the current events in the system, and the default includes columns for device, component, event class, summary, first time, last time, count, and event log. We can change the fields displayed in the view through the Event Manager, which we will cover later in this chapter. From the Event Console, we can navigate to the device overview page by clicking on the device name in the column. We can also navigate to the event class overview by clicking on the class name in the event class column.

By default, the Event Console displays events with a minimum severity of information and minimum state of acknowledged with filters to expand or restrict the view. To filter by severity or state, select a new value from the list in the table header and the Event Console automatically updates. The following table illustrates the available severities from the least to the most severe with a brief description of how they may be used. There are no hard and fast rules to dictate how we apply event severities to our system.

Event Severity	Description
Clear	Correlates to a previous down event and moves the event to history.
Debug	Used for troubleshooting. Does not indicate a problem.
Info	Used to mark an event in the system for informational purposes.
Warning	Indicates a potential problem.
Error	The device or component is unavailable or is operating at dangerous performance levels.
Critical	The device or component is down.

Event states categorize the current status of an event. The following table lists the event states with a brief description of the state:

Event State	Description
Suppressed	An event occurred, but it was sent directly to history.
Acknowledged	The event is still active and is being worked on by an admin.
Unacknowledged	Represents a new event that has not been acknowledged and is presumably not being worked on.

If we want to monitor the **Event Console** in real time and make the view automatically update when a new event occurs, click the Start link in the table header. The Start label turns to **Stop**, and the **Event Console** refreshes every 60 seconds.

The Event Console search box enables us to search for text in any of the displayed table columns. For example, if we want to view all the events in the Unknown event class, we can search for "**unknown**" (refer to the screenshot below).

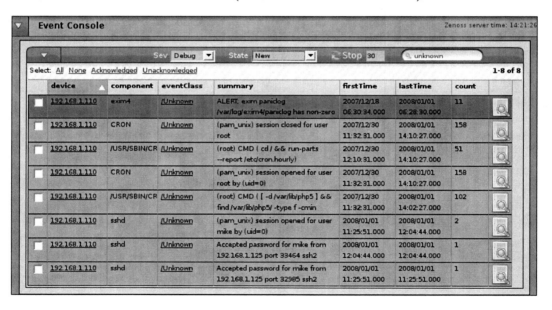

Event Log

We access the event log by clicking on the magnifying glass icon in the Event Console. The log consists of three tabs: **Fields**, **Details**, and **Log**. The **Fields** tab (as shown in the following screenshot) provides a list of all the fields we could possibly display in the Event Console view. If Zenoss knows the value of a field, it's populated. Refer to Appendix A for a list of event fields and their meaning.

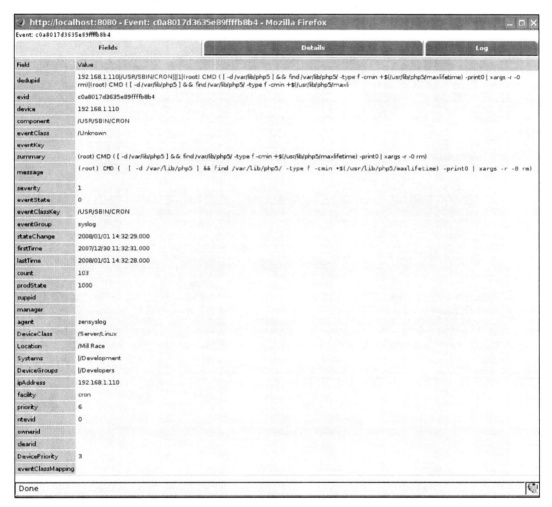

The **Details** tab of the event log (refer to following screenshot) shows additional event information, but there are no defined list of fields that display on this tab. Some Zenoss daemons automatically log information to the details field, such as the process ID of a syslog event.

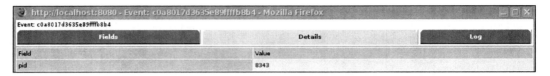

The final tab of the Event Log is **Log** (as seen in the following screenshot) , which administrators can use to record the notes relevant to the event. Type a message in the text box and click the **Add Message** button to create a log entry. Zenoss records the time stamp of the entry, the **User** who created the entry, and the **Text** of the entry.

We talk more about user management in chapter 9, but identifiying which user created a log entry is just one reason why we want to work as a regular user versus working as the admin user. If everyone creates log entries as the admin user for an event, how can we determine who is working on resolving the event?

Device Event View

While the Event Console displays all events, we can also view events on a per device basis. If we select a device from the Device List and choose the **Events** tab, we see a list table that resembles the Event Console.

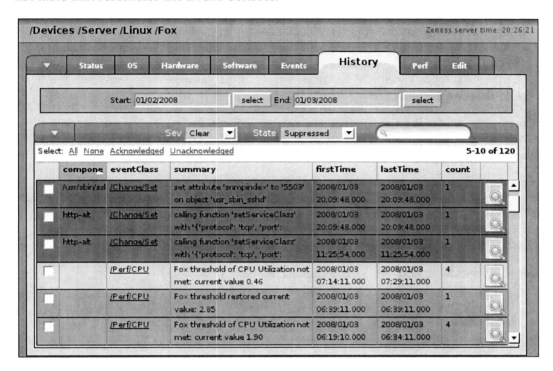

Click on the **History** tab to see yet another device view (as shown in the previous screenshot). The **History** tab interests us for two main reasons. First, we can limit the events we see by date range. Second, we can see all events including the events that have been automatically archived in history or suppressed.

Event Classes

Zenoss maps events to classes, which has a hierarchy of properties similar to the device, service, and process classes we looked at in earlier chapters. Zenoss generates events in response to some monitoring activity, which is why we have the ability to assign multiple severities to events. Zenoss evaluates the details of the monitoring activity that caused an event to see if it can match the details to an event instance. The event instance maps the event to a class via an event class key. More than one event class key can exist, which allows us to assign an order of precedence to how each event instance is mapped to event classes. We'll examine the event evaluation procedure later in this section.

After the event maps to an event class, Zenoss assigns the class' zProperties to the event. Next, the event inherits the device's properties. After the device details are processed, Zenoss updates the event to reflect the new properties.

For example, let's say we configure the /Status/IpService event class to have a fail severity equal to error. We then set /IpService/Privileged/ssh service class to a fail severity equal to critical. Based on the hierarchical event processing, all IpServices, such as SMTP, fail with a severity of error. However, if the SSH service fails, the event inherits the service class properties and fails with a critical severity.

Let's take a look around the Event Class screens.

Classes

From the navigation panel, select Events to display the Events Classes page. The Classes page shows summary information for Status, SubClasses, and Event Class Mappings.

The Status table shows the number of Events by severity, number of sub classes, and the number of event instances. The SubClasses table shows the number of classes, number of event Instances, and number of Events per class organizer. The EventClass Mappings table lists the event instance names along with the Evaluation description and number of active Events per mapping.

We drill down an event class hierarchy by clicking on the subclass name and the details we see on the screen are based on the position in the event hierarchy from which we are viewing. So, if we view the top level Events class, the status page indicates that we have 130 subclasses and 336 event instances. When we click on the **App** name from the SubClasses table, the status reflects **16** subclasses and **70** event instances (see following screenshot).

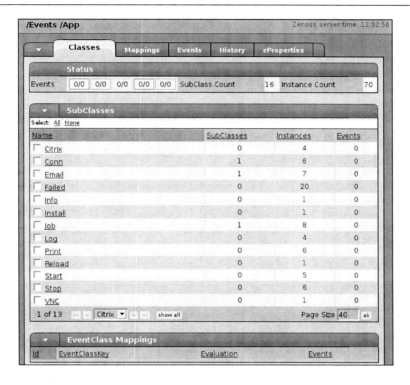

We can add, delete, and move the SubClass organizers and EventClass Mappings from the applicable table menu.

Mappings

The Mappings tab displays each mapping rule for the event class along with the associated event class, evaluation rule, and the number of active events for the mapping. Let's take a closer look at the Heartbeat event class mappings. From the navigation menu, select **Events**. Then select Heartbeat from the SubClasses table and choose the **Mappings** tab (see following screenshot).

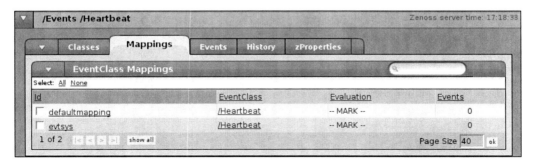

We can add, delete, and move mappings from the table menu, but for now, we'll edit an existing mapping. From the **EventClass Mappings** table, click on **evtsys** to display the property tabs. We see some familiar tabs along with some new tabs. The zProperties, Events, History, and Modifications tabs work the same way as they do for the parent event class, so we'll focus on the Status, Edit, and Sequence tab.

Status

The **Status** page that is displayed when we edit the evtsys mapping provides a summary of the event class mapping. Remember, screens within Zenoss are context sensitive, which means that the status overview we see shows the number of events that apply to the selected event class mapping.

The **EventClassInst** table provides a read-only view of the event mapping rules (refer to the following screenshot). We modify the event mapping rules in the **Edit** tab.

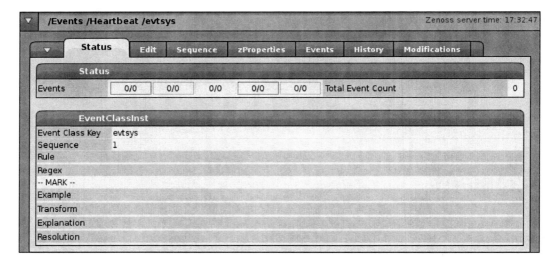

Edit

On the Edit tab, we have several text boxes that we use to define the mapping rules (see the following screenshot).

Our evtsys event class mapping is a relatively simple example. If the details of an event match the text "**-- Mark --**", Zenoss applies the evtsys zProperties to the event. The following table outlines the available text boxes on the **Edit** tab.

Option	Description
Name	A descriptive name for the event class mapping.
Event Class Key	Maps the event to the event class. More than one class can have the same Event Class Key.
Sequence	Defines the order in which the Event Class Key is processed in relation to the other keys with the same name.
Rule	A Python expression that evaluates the current event using the evt environment variable and an event field. For example: evt.ipAddress == 192.168.1.132
Regex	A regular expression used to match the current event details.
Example	Sample event text. Click Save to validate the regular expression against the Example text. If the Regex command turns red, the expression does not match the Example.
Transform	Enter TALES expressions to manipulate the event. For example: evt.summary = 'Change the event summary'. For more information about TALES expressions, see Appendix B.
Explanation	A text description of the mapping rules.
Resolution	Provides details to resolve the event.

In order to apply the mapping to the event class, we need to specify a **Rule**, **Regex**, or **Transform** command. Don't forget to **Save** changes when you finish.

Sequence

Each event mapping can have multiple instances that map events to different event classes, and to demonstrate, we continue using our evtsys event class mapping example. Click on the **Sequence** tab to display all the available instances of the mapping.

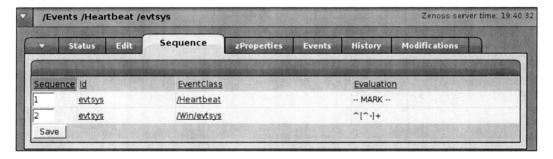

The **Sequence** page (as shown in the previous screenshot) displays the **Sequence, ID**, **EventClass**, and **Evaluation** for each instance of the event class mapping. In our example, we learn how we can map events in evtsys maps to the /Heartbeat and the /Win/evtsys classes.

The **Sequence** number determines the order in which each instance is processed. By default, the evtsys instance for the **/Heartbeat** event class gets processed first. If the regular expression "-- MARK --" is found in the event details, Zenoss maps the event to the **/Heartbeat** class and stops processing. If the "-- MARK --" regular expression is not matched, then the second instance of evtsys is processed.

To change the order in which the event class mappings get processed, enter the new sequence and click **Save**.

Events And History

Let's navigate back to the top level /Events class and select the Events tab. The Events tab has the same look and feel as the Event Console. If we sit at the top level of the /Events class, we see all the active events in the system just like the Event Console. As we navigate an event class hierarchy, the Events tab filters the list to show only the events in the current event class and below.

To view the event history for an event class, click the History tab, and like the Event Console, we can filter the events by date range.

zProperties

After an event maps to an event class, the class **zProperties** are assigned. If the event class mapping has different zProperties set, the event inherits the zProperties of the event class mapping.

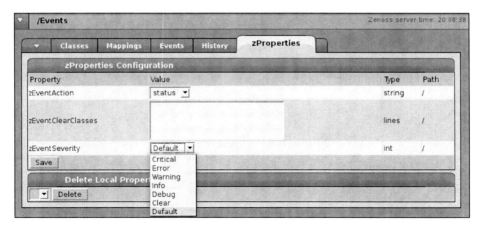

The available **zProperties** (shown in the previous screenshot) are outlined in the following table:

zProperty	Description
zEventAction	Specify the action to take on the event. The following options are available: • Status — Keep the event active and display it in the Event Console. • History — Move the event straight to history. Does not show the event on the Event Console. • Drop — Do not archive the event.
zEventClearClasses	Clear the event if the the device generates an event that matches one of the specified event classes.
zEventSeverity	Specify the fail severity for the event. In descending order of severity, the available options are: • **Critical** • **Error** • **Warning** • **Info** • **Debug** • **Clear** • **Default**

Event Manager

The Event Manager provides an interface that allows us to configure how events are stored, displayed, and acted on. We access the Event Manager from the navigation panel.

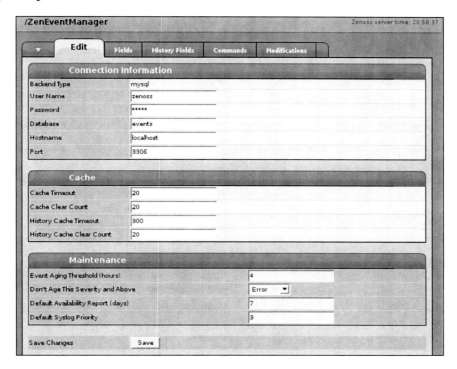

The **Edit** tab displays when we first open the Event Manager and provides three configuration areas: **Connection Information**, **Cache**, and **Maintenance** (as shown in the previous screenshot). The following fields are available:

Field	Description
Connection Information	
Backend Type	Specify the database type. Only **MySQL** is available.
User Name	Database user name. Default is "**zenoss**."
Password	Password for user name. Default is "**zenoss**."
Database	Events database name. Default is "**events**."
Host name	Database host name. Default is "**localhost**."
Port	Database port number. Default is **3306**.

Field	Description
Cache	
Cache Timeout	Sets the event cache timeout in seconds. The lower the number, the more responsive the Event Console will be. The default is 20.
Cache Clear Count	Sets a threshold to clear event cache counts. The default is 20.
History Cache Timeout	Sets the history event cache timeout in seconds. The lower the number, the more responsive the history events views will be. The default is 300.
History Cache Clear Count	Sets a threshold to clear history event cache counts. The default is 20.
Maintenance	
Event Aging Threshold (hours)	If the event has not been acknowledged in the specified amount of time, move it to history. Default is **4** hours.
Don't Age This Severity and Above	Events higher than the specified severity will not automatically go to history. Default is "**error.**"
Default Availability Report (days)	Specify the number of days to show data for the availability report. The default is **7**.
Default Syslog Priority	Monitor syslog events with the specified syslog priority and above. The default is **3**, which is the error.

Don't forget to click **Save** after making any changes.

Fields

The Fields tab of the Event Manager provides a way to add and remove fields from the Event Console and from a device's Event tab. The page divides into two rows: **Default Result Fields** and **Device Result Fields** (refer to the next screenshot). The assigned fields display in the left column for each row.

If we remember the collector plug-in section of Chapter 5, these page controls look familiar. To remove a field from the assigned column, click the "x" next to the field name. To add fields, click the **Add Fields** link to display a list of available fields. Then drag them to the left column to assign them.

The fields assigned to the **Default Result Fields** display on the Event Console and the Events tab of the Event Class. The fields assigned to the **Device Result Fields** display on the device's Events tab.

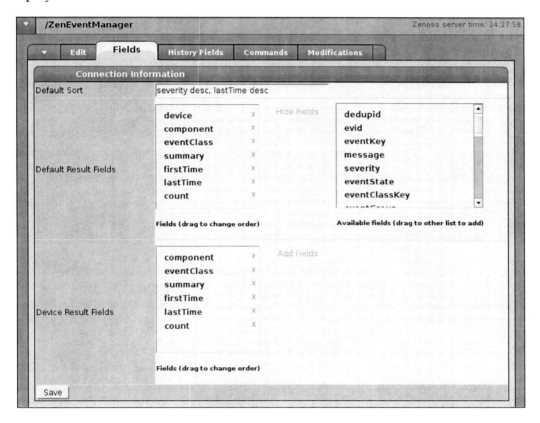

The **History Fields** tab provides the same field assignment options as the **Fields** tab. The fields assigned to the Default Result Fields display on the event class' History tab, while the fields assigned to the Device Result Fields display on the device's History tab.

Both the **Fields** and the **History Fields** pages provide a Default Sort field to control how the data is sorted. The default sort order for the **Fields** tab is descending by severity, then descending by last time. The **History Fields** sort descending by last time.

The syntax for the sort field is to list the field name to be sorted followed by the sort order. Multiple sort conditions (fields) are separated by a comma, as illustrated in the **Fields** tab. If we want to sort our historical events in ascending order by count, we enter "count asc" as the **Default Sort**.

Commands

Through the **Commands** tab of the Event Manager (shown in the following screenshot), we can create shell commands run on the Zenoss server based on an event. We'll create a simple command to write to a file.

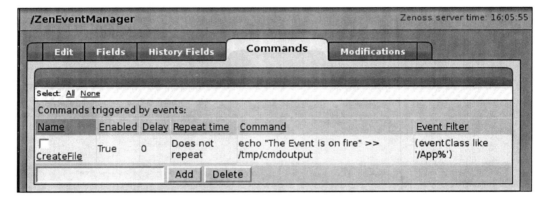

The Commands table lists each defined command by name with an overview of the commands properties. To create a command, type a descriptive name (e.g: **CreateFile**) in the text box and click the **Add** button. Click on the command name to display the Edit tab.

The following table lists each of the options on the command's edit tab.

Property	Description
Enabled	Select True to enable the command and False to disable it.
Default Command Timeout	The time in seconds to wait for the command to complete. The default is 60.
Delay	The time in seconds Zenoss waits to execute the command from the time an event triggers the command. The default is 0.
Repeat Time	Repeat the command once in every specified interval. The default is 0 seconds.

Property	Description
Command	Enter the command to run when a new event matches the command filter. Accepts either Python or TALES expressions.
Clear Command	Enter the command to run when a clear event matches the command filter. Accepts Python or TALES expressions.
Where	Add filters to modify the conditions that trigger the command.

Let's modify our CreateFile command in the following way. Set the Enabled field to True. In the Command field, enter the following:

```
echo "The Event with ID ${evt/evid} is on fire!" >> /tmp/
SampleEventCommand
```

In the Clear Command field, enter the following:

```
echo "${evt/evid} for ${dev/id} is no longer a burning issue" >> /tmp/
SampleEventCommand
```

In the Where field, define a filter for Event Class that begins with /App. Save the changes.

The following screenshot shows the result of the CreateFile command for both new and clear events.

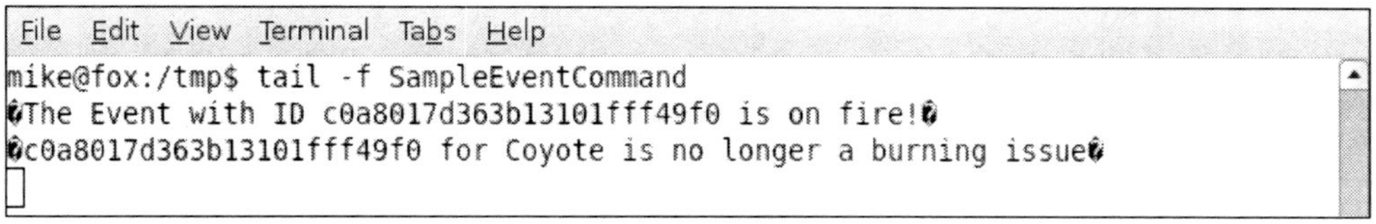

We will discuss ways to test events in the Add Events section of this chapter.

Working with Events

So far in this chapter, we've taken a look at events from several different angles, and we have a good understanding about how events work in Zenoss. For the most part, the event creation process is automatic, and we don't need to think about it, but Zenoss provides us with several mechanisms that allows us to interact with events. We will learn how to manually add events for troubleshooting purposes, map events, view overridden objects, can transform events.

Add Events

We have three ways to test our event rules:

- We wait for the device to go down.
- We make the device go down.
- We take a less intrusive approach and manually create events without imposing any down time on the device.

We add events from the page menu of the event class.

If we navigate to the event class we want to create an event for, Zenoss automatically populates the Event Class with the selected class. We'll continue working with the CreateFile command we created earlier in the Chapter.

To add an event and test our event command (refer to the next screenshot):

1. Navigate to the /App event class.
2. Select Add Event from the page menu.
3. Enter a **Message**.
4. Enter a device name (for example, **Coyote**).
5. Select **Severity** equal to **Critical**.
6. Select **/App** for the **Event Class**.

7. Click **OK**.

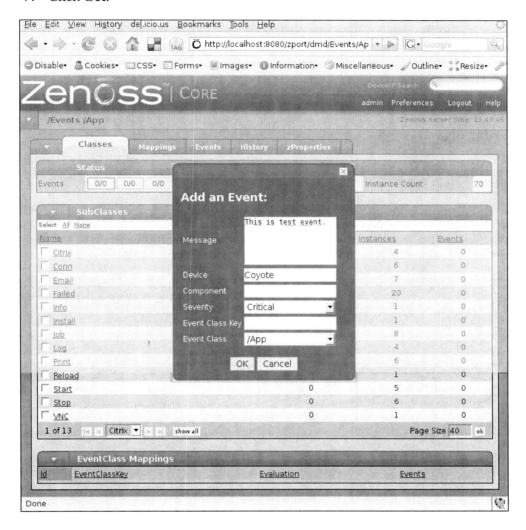

The event we just created displays in the Event Console and in the Events tab of the /Events/App class. Now, check the /tmp/SampleEventCommand file we created in the event command section earlier in the Chapter and verify if the event created an entry in the file.

Next, we simulate a clear event. Add another event for Coyote in the /App event class, but this time choose Clear for the Event Severity. When we send the clear event, Zenoss correlates the event and moves it to history. All the event views update to reflect the new event status and the /tmp/Sample/Event/Command file is updated based on the clear command we specified in the CreateFile command.

We can review both events from the History tab. Let's open the event log for the down event we created. Scroll to the bottom of the Fields tab and note that Zenoss has populated the deletedTime and clearid fields with the information from the clear event. Click over to the Log tab, and we see a log entry by the admin user with the text "auto cleared." The value in the Date field matches the deletedTime value on the Fields tab.

As long as we know the specific event condition we want to test, we can use the add event option to simulate a real event, thereby allowing use to test mapping rules, event commands, or notification rules.

Map Events

Sometimes Zenoss receives an event that it cannot map to an event class, so it maps it to the /Unknown event class. Syslog events, for example, map to the /Unknown event class. A quick look at the **History** tab (see the following screenshot) for the **/Events** class shows several **unknown** events for our Zenoss system.

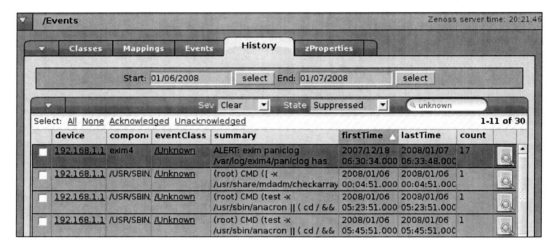

If we need more details on an unknown event, we can review the event log to determine the component, event group, Zenoss agent, and other device organization information. If we want to map an event that has already been archived to the history, we must select the event and select Undelete Events from the History table menu.

Let's take an example where we have an active event from an exim4 mail server program event which we want to map to the /App/Log event class (refer to the following screenshot).

To map the event:

1. Select the event from the Events list.
2. Select Map Events to Class from the table menu.
3. In the Map Events dialog box, select the event class (e.g., /App/Log).
4. Click OK to map the event to an event class.

After we map the event, Zenoss displays the event mapping Status tab, which we covered earlier in the chapter. By default, no commands are defined in the **Rule**, **Regex**, or **Transform** options, but the summary of the alert is automatically populated into the **Example** field (refer to the following screenshot) which helps validate any regular expressions we define.

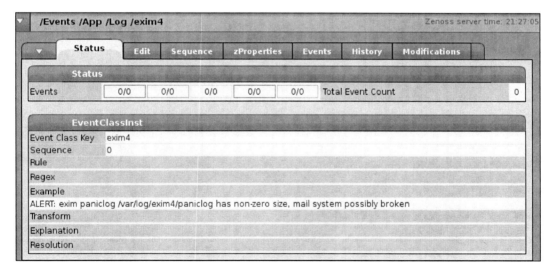

Let's test our mapping by adding a new event following the steps in the preceding Add Event section. Give the event the following attributes:

- Message: This is a test event
- Device: Any device
- Event Class Key: exim4
- Event Class: Leave blank

The event displays in the Event Console. To clear the event, we can send a clear event, or we can move it to history. To move an event to history:

1. Select the event from the Event Console.
2. Select Move to History from the page menu.
3. Click OK to confirm the move.

If the event class we want to map the event to does not exist, we create the event class by adding a new event class organizer. We can create as many subclass organizers as we need to identify an event hierarchy, or we can add a new subclass organizer into an existing event class structure.

In addition to adding new classes, we can add new mappings. To add a new event mapping:

1. Select Events from the navigation menu.
2. Navigate to the event class we want to add the mapping to (e.g., /App/Log).
3. Select Add Mapping from the EventClass Mappings table menu.
4. In the Add Event Class Mappings dialog box, enter a descriptive name.
5. Click OK to add the mapping.

Now we can edit the mapping to add rules to map the event to a class and zProperties to handle the event.

Overridden Objects

Sometimes our events do not process as we expect them to process because Zenoss allows us to customize our event rules in the class hierarchies and for individual devices. To help track down problems with our event processing rules, we can view the overridden objects. Overridden objects are the classes and event class mappings that have custom zProperties.

To display the overridden objects, open the Events Class and select More > Overridden Objects from the page menu. The **Overriding Objects** table provides a **zProperty** selection that corresponds to the available zProperties for an event: **zEventAction**, zEventClearClasses, and zEventSeverity. To filter the list, select a zProperty.

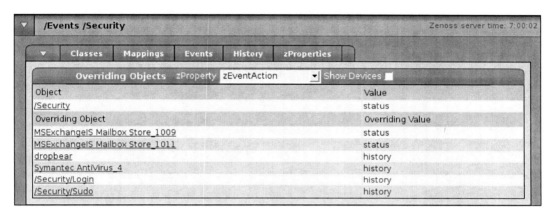

The first listing in the table is the **Object** and its default **Value**. The table then lists the **Overriding Objects** with the **Overriding Values**. In Zenoss, the **Overriding Value** takes precedence and is where we want to go to make changes. Objects, in this context, refer to both event classes and mappings. Click on the object name to edit the object's zProperties.

Transformations

Event transformations occur in two locations. We already reviewed transformations at the event class mapping level. We can also define transformations at the event class level. Transformations use TALES expressions to change the event details as the event is processed.

To create an event transformation:

1. Navigate to the event class we want to transform.

2. Select **More > Transform** from the page menu.

3. Enter a Python statement to process the event.

The following screen capture shows an event transformation that changes the event state for device Master to acknowledged (1) for the /Status/Wmi/Conn event class.

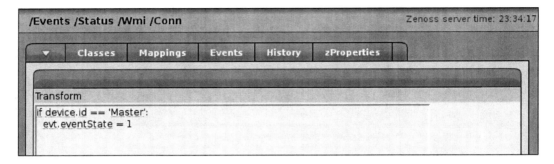

Zenoss provides a modified Python shell named zendmd that lets us interact with the Zenoss object database. We can use zendmd to test our python statements and to access the methods and attributes available to us from Zenoss. We'll review zendmd in Chapter 10.

Event Work Flow

When Zenoss creates an event that requires action, the event displays on the Event Console. As we've seen, some events are information only and can be sent straight to history, while other events clear themselves; however, when an event pops up on the event console, it needs attention.

Our first step is to acknowledge the event from the Event Console. To acknowledge an event, select it from the list, and choose Acknowledge Event from the table menu. The event turns a lighter shade to visually indicate that someone has acknowledged the event (see the next screenshot). The event is still active, so it continues to display in the Event Console.

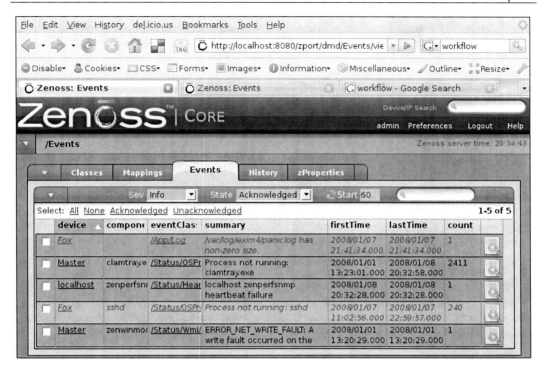

Our second step is to open the Event Log and add an entry to the Log tab to let others know that the event is being worked on. After we resolve the event, we can add another Log entry to specify the resolution.

The third step clears the event. To clear the event, choose the event from the Event Console and select Move to History from the table menu. Alternatively, we can let Zenoss automatically detect that the device is up and let it clear the event via up/down event correlation.

Event De-Duplication

If we have a web server down, Zenoss continues to monitor it every 60 seconds and will continue to generate an event each time it determines that the web server is down. That comes to 1,440 events a day. Thankfully, Zenoss suppresses all that noise with event de-duplication.

If Zenoss determines that the event is a duplicate of an existing event, it increments the event count, rather than generate a new event. As we will see in Chapter 9, events trigger alerts, and by suppressing duplicate events, we avoid duplicate alerts for active events, thereby reducing alert chatter. The de-duplication identification (dedupid) is set to device, component, event class, event key, and severity.

Summary

Zenoss provides a wealth of information about our networks and systems in the form of events. Using the event management concepts in this Chapter, we can utilize that information to manage our IT resources in a way that meets our individual needs. We can now move around the Event Console and multiple event views to interact with active and archived events. We can collect syslog messages and monitor Windows Event Log. We know how to customize our event processing rules by running event-triggered commands, mapping events, and transforming events.

In the next chapter, we shift from working an event or a device in real time to a historical view that lets us examine all the events and devices in relation to each other via the Zenoss reports. Then we'll move into administering the Zenoss system, including user management and alerts.

8
System Reports

Zenoss Core includes several reports that allow us to aggregate device, event, performance, and user data into single views. Until now, we have spent all our time reviewing information at a per device, per component, or per class level, but the reports present a broad view of our IT resources in the context of all the devices, components, or classes.

In this chapter, we'll review each of the included reports, as well as create a custom multi-graph report.

Report Overview

To see a list of the default organizers, select **Reports** from the navigation menu. The report organizers we will cover are:

- **Device Reports**
- **Event Reports**
- **Graph Reports**
- **Multi-Graph Reports**
- **Performance Reports**

- **User Reports**

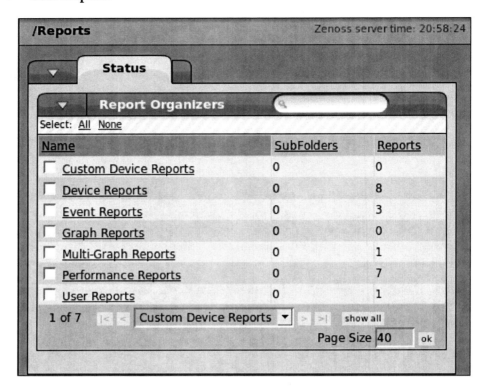

Next to each organizer name (see the previous screenshot), we see the list of **Subfolders** or suborganizers and the number of **Reports** included in each organizer. Like many things in Zenoss, we have the ability to add and remove organizers to create a custom report hierarchy.

We can then navigate up and down the hierarchy to display the available reports. Displaying a report is as simple as clicking on the report name from the current report organizer.

Many reports, except graphs, provide a search field in the report heading which we can use to filter the contents of the report. The filter searches each column in the report for a match. Each report has an export option that saves the report data in a comma separated value (csv) format according to the applied filter.

Device Reports

The Device Reports organizer contains reports that aggregate information from all
the devices in the Zenoss inventory and provides the following reports:

- All Devices
- All Monitored Devices
- Device Changes
- Model Collection Age
- New Devices
- Ping Status Issues
- SNMP Status Issues
- Software Inventory

All Devices

The **All Devices** report (refer to the following screenshot) lists each device from the
inventory by **Name** with additional columns for **Class**, **Product**, **State**, **Ping** status,
and **SNMP** status.

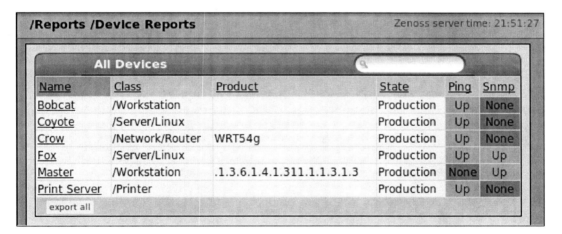

At one point or another, we have touched on each one of the columns displayed
on the report, except **Product**. The **Product** column shows the hardware product
description from the device's Edit tab.

Manufacturers and Products

Zenoss includes a products class that organizes by manufacturers with products as subclasses. If we click on the Products menu from the navigation panel, a list of manufacturers is displayed (as shown in the following screenshot) with familiar names, such as **Apple, Cisco**, and **Microsoft**.

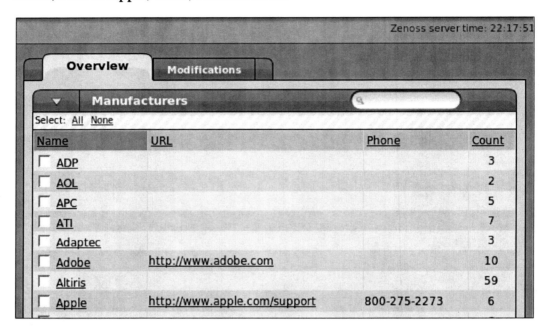

The **Manufacturers** table displays the URL, the **Phone** number, and a **Count** of the products included for each manufacturer. Click on the name of a manufacturer to edit the organizer's properties and see the list of products. The **Overview** page (see the following screenshot) displays the manufacturer's contact information, including his web site **URL, Phone**, and address. We can modify the contact information as necessary from the **Edit** tab.

The **Products** table displays a list of products that belong to the manufacturer with columns for **Type, Product Key**, and **Count**. The available types are **Operating System, Hardware**, and software. The **Product Key** identifies the product, and the **Count** column shows the total number of devices assigned to the product.

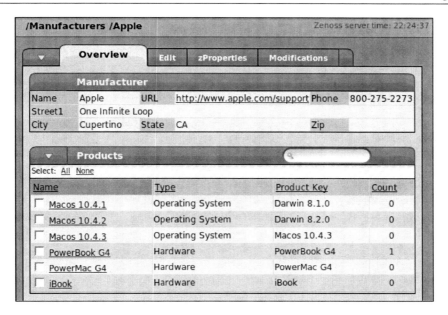

Click on a product name to display its **Overview** page (refer to the following screenshot). We see the product configuration information in the **Product** table, as well as a **Description** field and **Part Number** field. All the values can be modified from the **Edit** tab.

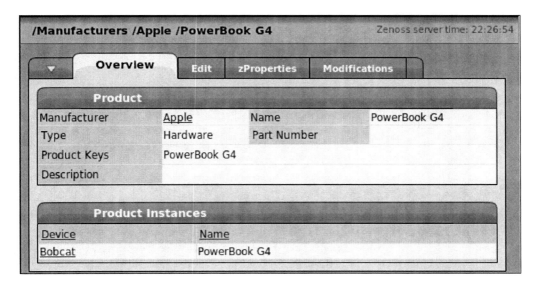

The **Product Instances** table lists the name of the devices currently attached to the product. If we click on the device name, the device's status page loads.

All Monitored Components

The **All Monitored Components** report lists all the interfaces, processes, services, file systems, and routes that are being monitored for each device. The information contained in the report correlates to the OS tab for each device. The following screenshot shows the All Monitored Components report sorted by device.

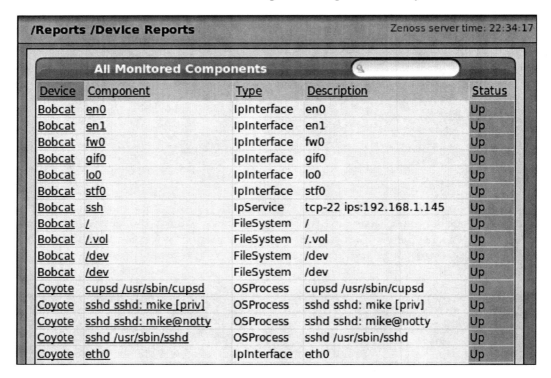

The report includes the **Device** name, **Component** name, **Type**, **Description**, and component **Status**. Click on the device name to view the device's status page or click on the component name to view the properties screen for the component.

Device Changes

When Zenoss models a device and detects a change, it records the date of the change. The **Device Changes** report displays all devices that have changed within the past day (see the following screenshot). The report lists the device by **name** and **class**. We also see the date and time when the device was **First Seen**, last modeled, and changed.

Model Collection Age

If a device's model has a production state higher than 0 and has not been updated for 48 hours, it displays on the Model Collection Age report. The report includes the same data as the Device Changes report: Name, class, first seen, collection, and change. Devices that have the zProperty zSnmpMonitorIgnore set to True are excluded.

New Devices

The New Devices report shows a list of devices that have been added to the Zenoss inventory within the past seven days. The report lists the device class and timestamps for the first seen, collection, and change dates.

Ping Status Issues

The Ping Status report (see the following screenshot) shows a list of devices that currently have a ping status other than up. In addition to the device **Name** and **Class**, the report lists the hardware **Product** description, **State**, **Ping** status, and **SNMP** status. If the ping status is down, a count of failed ping attempts is displayed in the **Ping** status column.

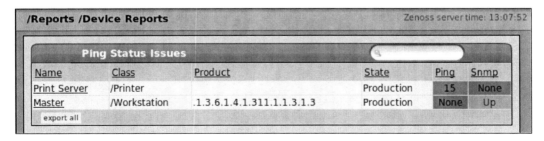

SNMP Status Issues

The **SNMP Status Issues** report is similar to the Ping Status Issues report, except that it reports devices that have an **SNMP** status other than up. For devices that have an SNMP status equal to down, Zenoss reports the number of failures.

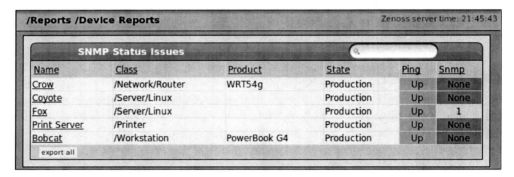

Software Inventory

The **Software Inventory** report pulls data from two sources and organizes the information by manufacturer and product. If we specify an OS Manufacturer and OS Product on a device's Edit tab, that selection displays on the report. The report also includes the software listed on the device's Software tab. The **Count** column on the report provides the total number of instances that the software product shows up in the device inventory.

/Reports /Device Reports
Zenoss server time: 21:59:2

Software Inventory

Manufacturer	Product	Count
Ubuntu	7.04	1
Adobe	Adobe Reader 7.0	1
Google	Google Toolbar for Internet Explorer	1
HP	HP Software Update	1
Sun	J2SE Runtime Environment 5.0 Update 2	1
Microsoft	Microsoft .NET Framework 1.1	2
Microsoft	Microsoft .NET Framework 2.0	2
Microsoft	Microsoft ActiveSync 3.7	1
Microsoft	Microsoft Office XP Professional	1
Microsoft	Microsoft Windows XP	1
Snmp-Informant	SNMP Informant Agent _Standard Edition	1
Microsoft	Security Update for Windows Media Player _KB911564	1
Microsoft	Security Update for Windows XP _KB890046	1
Microsoft	Security Update for Windows XP _KB893756	1

If we click on the manufacturer link, the manufacturer overview page is displayed with information specific to the vendor, including associated products. If we click on the product name, the product overview page is displayed and we see a list of all the devices associated with the product.

Event Reports

The event reports give us a system-wide view of event classes, mappings, and heartbeats. We'll review the following reports:

- All Event Classes
- All Event Mappings
- All Heartbeats

All Event Classes

To see a list of all the event classes defined in the system, we view the **All Event Classes** report. For each event class, the report includes the number of **Subclasses**, **Instances** of the class within the system, and the number of current system **Events**.

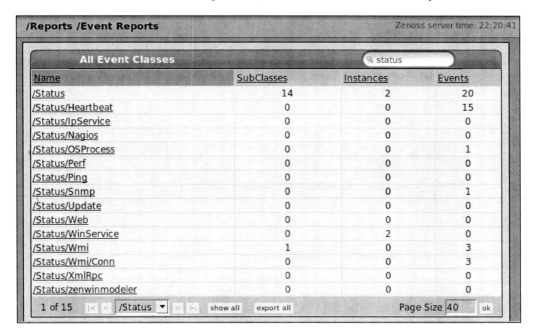

All Event Mappings

The **All Event Mappings** report displays a list of all the event mappings currently defined in the Zenoss system. For each event mapping, the report lists the **EventClassKey**, the **Evaluation** text, and the number of current system **Events**.

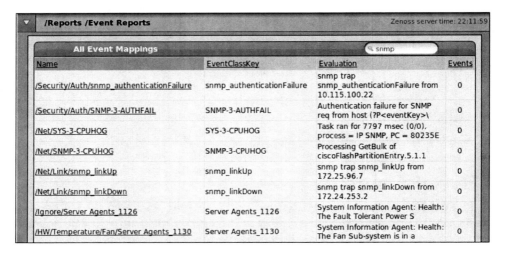

All Heartbeats

Heartbeats monitor the health of the Zenoss daemons, and the All Heartbeats report displays the list of current heartbeat failures by **Device** and **Component**. On the report, the **Components** column corresponds to the available daemons, such as **zenactions** and **zenstatus**. The report provides the duration of the heartbeat failure in **Seconds**.

Device	Component	Seconds
localhost	zenmodeler	2763
localhost	zenperfsnmp	203
localhost	zenprocess	71
localhost	zenactions	59
localhost	zenping	30
localhost	zenwin	29
localhost	zeneventlog	28
localhost	zenwinmodeler	27
localhost	zenstatus	17
localhost	zensyslog	14
localhost	zentrap	11
localhost	zencommand	2
Fox	zenping	2650922
Fox	zenstatus	2650920
Fox	zenactions	2650914

Graph Reports

Graph reports allow us to create custom graphs based on the existing performance graphs for interfaces, processes, file systems, memory, and CPU. Let's take file systems as an example of what we can do with a graph report. If we recall our discussion about performance graphs in Chapter 6, we know that we can view graphs for each volume on a per device basis by going to the OS tab and clicking on the mount point name for each device.

By creating a graph report, we can create one view with multiple, related graphs. For example, if we want to see file system graphs for all our file servers, we can create a graph to show us the relevant file systems from each file server.

Depending on our monitoring setup, Zenoss graphs the file system utilization for each volume on our devices. To see the information about a volume, we can go to the OS tab for a device and drill down on the volume name to get the graph, but we cannot compare these graphs with related servers. By creating a graph report, we can display multiple, related graphs in one view.

Zenoss does not include any graph reports by default. Let's build a custom report to monitor a file system on our test server Fox:

1. Select **Reports** from the navigation menu.
2. Select the **Graph Reports** organizer.
3. From the **Reports** table menu, select **Add Graph Report**.
4. Enter a descriptive name (for example, File System Utilization on Backup Servers) in the ID field of the **Add Graph Report** dialog box.
5. Click **OK** to add the report and display the graph's Edit tab.
6. Select Fox from the list of devices in the Add New Graph table.
7. Select /media/disk from the component list.
8. Select Utilization from the list of graphs.
9. Click the Add Graph to Report button to save the graph.

The Edit tab contains all the settings we need to build our graph and is divided into three tables: Graph Report, Add New Graph, and Graphs. Our step-by-step instructions cover the fields required to add the graph, but let's review each section in more detail.

The Graph Report table includes descriptive information including **Name**, **Title**, **Number** of **Columns**, and **Comments** (as shown in the following screenshot). The value we enter for **Name** displays on both the onscreen and printed version of the graph. The **Comments** field provides a mix of HTML and TALES expressions to add a report description to the printed version of the graph, which defaults to the Zenoss logo, and report date and time.

Zenoss uses Zope's Template Attribute Language Expression Syntax (TALES) throughout the system to report on events and devices. Appendix B provides more information about TALES. For now, we'll leave the comment section as-is.

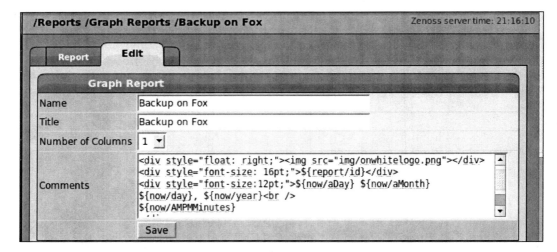

In the **Add New Graph** table, we have **Device**, **Component**, and **Graph** selection boxes (see the following screenshot). The component selections depend on the selected device, and the available graphs depend on the selected components. If no graphs get displayed, then the selected component does not have a graph and we need to choose a different component.

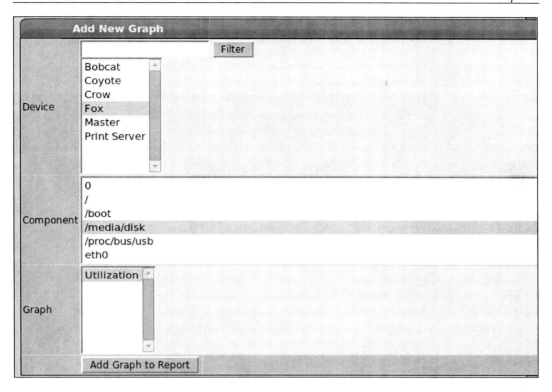

After we click the **Add Graph to Report** button, the graph displays in the **Graphs** table. We can add as many graphs as we need. In the **Graphs** table, we see the report's summary information, including **Sequence** number, **Name**, **Device**, **Component**, and **Graph** type (see the following screenshot).

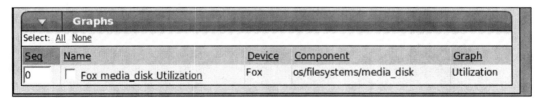

If we add more than one graph, we use the other sequence number to control the order in which the graphs are displayed on the screen. The name column lists the graph report element name and provides a hyperlink to edit the graph report element properties.

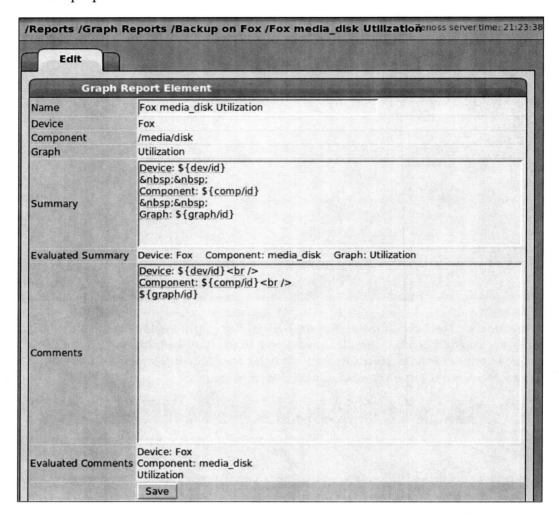

The important fields are **Summary** and **Comments** (see the previous screenshot). The **Summary** section contains TALES expressions that print summary data above the graph, including **Device**, **Component**, and **Graph** type. The TALES expressions in the comments section display the summary information for the graph on the printable version of the report.

To run our new report, navigate back to the Graph Reports organizer and click on the report name to display the graph. Click the printable button to open a print-ready copy of the graph in a new browser window (as seen in the following screenshot).

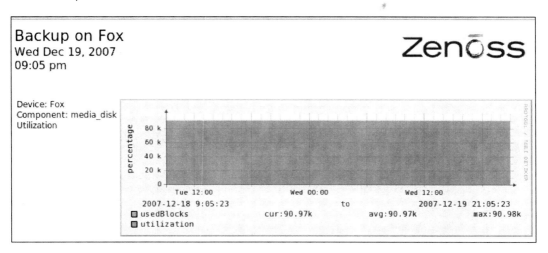

Multi-Graph Reports

Multi-graphs are similar to graph reports in that we define the devices and components to graph. Graph reports restrict us to existing performance graphs, whereas the multi-graph reports allow us to define our own data points. In addition, we can graph multiple devices and components on a single graph.

Let's add a multi-graph report that displays the interface 75% utilization threshold for all devices in the Mill Race location:

1. Select **Reports** from the navigation menu.

2. Select the **Multi-Graph Reports** organizer.

3. From the **Reports** table menu, select **Add Multi-Graph Reports**.

4. Enter a descriptive name (e.g: Interface Thresholds) in the ID field of the **Add Multi-Graph Report** dialog box.

5. Click OK to add the report and display the graph's **Edit** tab (see the following screenshot).

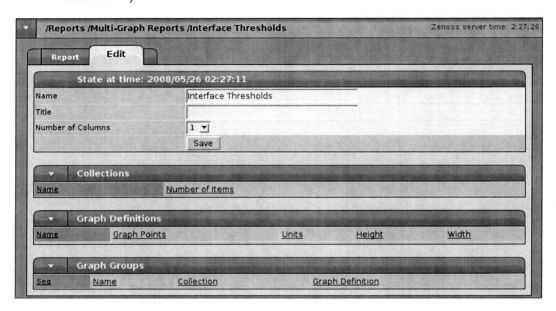

To finish setting up our multi-graph report, we need to add **Collections**, **Graph Definitions**, and **Graph Groups**. The **Collections** allow us to specify the list of devices we want to graph by device class, system, group, location, or specific device/component.

To add a new collection:

1. Select **Add Collection** from the Collections table menu.
2. Enter a descriptive name (for example, **Location**) in the ID field of the Add Collection dialog box.
3. Click OK to add the collection and display the properties.
4. In the **Add to Collection** table, select an **Item Type** (for example, Location).

5. From the list of available selections, select the item (for example, /Mill Race).

6. Set **Include Suborganizers** to **True** to recursively include all sub-organizers for the selected Item Type.

7. Click the **Add to Collection** button (see the following screenshot).

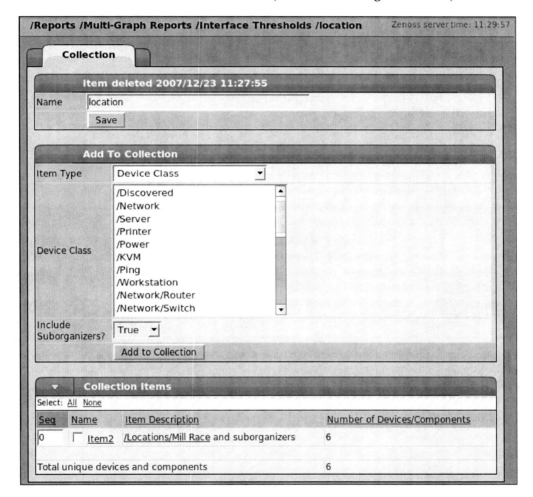

The **Collection Items** table updates to include a description of the item we added along with the number of devices selected. We can add as many item types to an individual collection as necessary, and we can add multiple collections.

Next, we add Graph Definitions to the report. Navigate back to the graph's Edit tab by clicking on the report name (for example, Interface Thresholds) in the breadcrumbs navigation:

1. Select Add Graph from the **Graph Definition** table menu.

2. Enter a descriptive name (e.g., Thresholds) in the ID field of the Add a New Graph dialog box.

3. Click OK to display the **Graph Definition** page.

4. From the **Graph Points** table menu, select Add Threshold.

5. In the **Add GraphPoint** dialog box, begin typing the threshold name to display a filtered list of graph points.

6. Select Utilization 75 perc.

7. Click OK to add the threshold to the Graph Points table.

The following screenshot shows the **Graph Definition** properties.

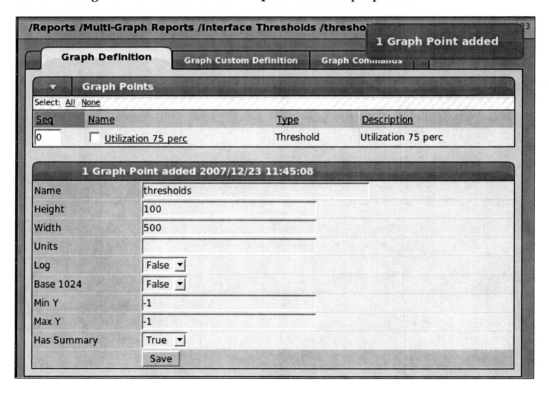

We can add multiple thresholds or data points to the graph definition, and we can have more than one graph definition per report. To add data points, select Add DataPoint from the **Graph Points** table menu. The Add DataPoint dialog box also filters the list of available data points as we type in the dialog box.

We can also change the way the graph displays by changing values such as height and width. We'll use the default values here.

Finally, we need to add a graph group. Navigate back to the report's Edit tab:

1. From the **Graph Groups** table menu, select **Add Graph Group**.

2. Enter a descriptive name in the ID field of the **Add Group dialog** box.

3. Click OK to display the Graph Group properties.

4. Select the **Collection** and **Graph Definition** to apply to the graph group (see the following screenshot).

5. In the **Method** drop-down list, choose one of the following values:

    *   Separate graph for each device
    *   **All devices on single graph**

6. Click **Save**.

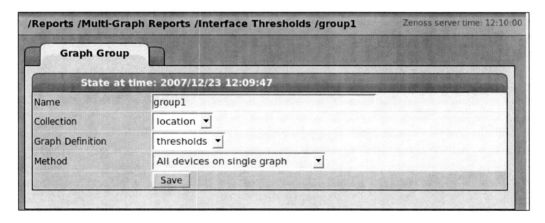

Our multi-graph example is simple in that we didn't add multiple collections and graph definitions; however, we have enough background to experiment with more complex multi-graphs to correlate device performance.

To view the multi-report, select the **Multi-Graph Reports** organizer from the Report page, then click on the report name.

Performance Reports

The performance reports include a mix of graphs and text-based reports:

- Aggregate
- Availability
- CPU Utilization
- Filesystem Utilization
- Interface Utilization
- Memory Utilization
- Threshold Summary

The aggregate report shows the performance graphs that combine data from all the devices into one graph for each measure, such as free memory.

Aggregate Reports

The available aggregate reports include CPU Use, Free Memory, Free Swap, and Network Input/Output for all the devices in the Zenoss inventory. We can customize how each graph is displayed by changing the graph parameters. To make changes, click on the graph image to open the parameters window (as shown in the following screenshot).

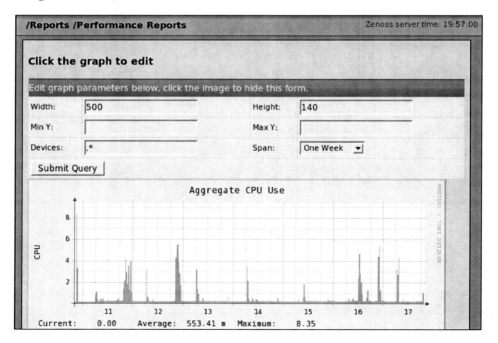

We can control the size of the graph by specifying a new **Width** and **Height** in pixels. In addition, we can set new minimum and maximum values for the y-axis that correspond to the unit of measurement for each graph. By default, all the devices are included, but we can view the graph for a single device by entering the device name in the **Devices** field.

The default time **Span** for the graph is **One Week**, but we may choose one day, two weeks, one month, or one year. After making the selections, press the **Submit Query** button, and Zenoss redraws the graph based on the new parameters.

Availability Report

The Availability report lists each device in the inventory along with its Systems organizer. The availability is calculated for the selected **Event Class** and **Severity**.

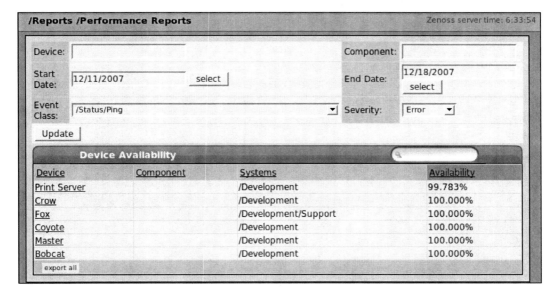

The default report gives us the availability percentage for the past seven days for the **/Status/Ping** event class with a **Severity** of **Error**. We can change the reporting criteria based on the following options:

Report Filter	Description
Device	Enter a device name to limit the report to a single device.
Component	Enter a component name from the device OS tab. Zenoss returns devices that match with the specified component.
Start Date	Specify the first day of the report.
End Date	Specify the last day of the report
Event Class	Select the type of the event to report on. For example: /Status/SNMP.
Severity	Select the event severity to use when calculating availability.

After we enter the report criteria, we can click on the **Update** button to view the new report.

CPU Utilization

The CPU Utilization provides the **Load Average** and the **Percent Utilization** for each device. If Zenoss is not collecting CPU performance statistics for a device, the **Load Average** and **Percent Utilization** values display as "**N/A**" (refer to the following screen capture).

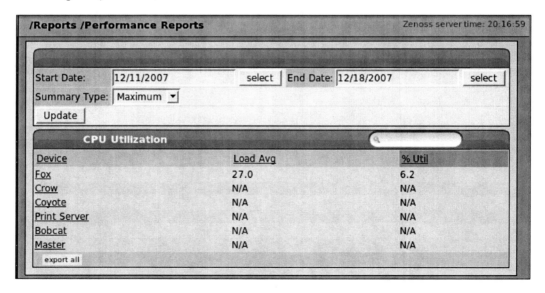

By default, the report displays for the previous seven days. However, we can specify custom **Start** and **End Dates** for the report. We can also choose one of the following **Summary Types**: **Maximum** or **Average**. **Maximum** displays the maximum **Load Average** and **Percent Utilization** for the date range while the average summary type provides average **Load Average** and **Percent Utilization** calculations.

Filesystem Utilization Report

All monitored file systems are included in the **Filesystem Utilization** report. For each file system **Mount** point, the report includes the **Device**, **Total Bytes**, **Used Bytes**, **Free Bytes**, and **Percent Utilization** (as seen in the next screenshot). If Zenoss does not know a value, it populates the report values with "**N/A**".

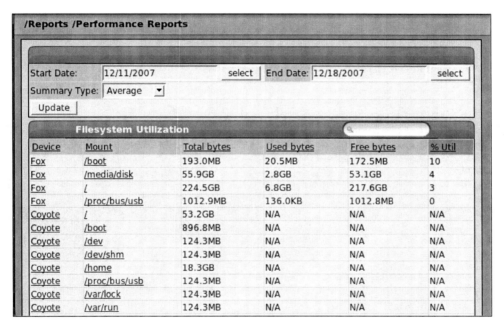

The default date range of the report includes the previous seven days, but we can specify our own **Start** and **End Dates**. We can further filter the report output by showing the maximum or Average usage statistics by choosing the appropriate option from the **Summary Type**.

Interface Utilization

The **Interface Utilization** Report (seen in the following screenshot) includes all monitored interfaces. For each **Interface**, the report includes the **Device, Speed, Input, Output, Total** throughput, and **Percent Utilization**. The report lists "**N/A**" for any unknown values.

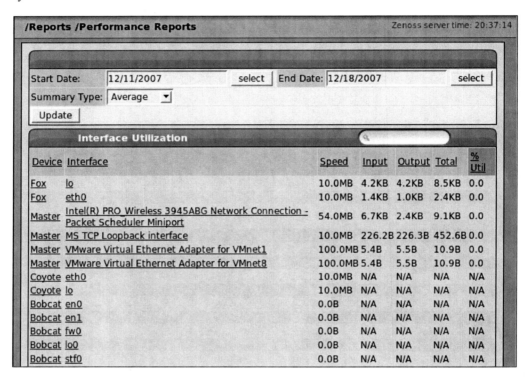

The default date range of the report includes the previous seven days, but we can specify our own **Start** and **End Dates**. We can further filter the report output by showing the maximum or Average usage statistics by choosing the appropriate option from the **Summary Type**.

Memory Utilization

The **Memory Utilization** Report (see the next screenshot) includes all the devices and provides the following memory statistics: **Total, Available, Cached, Buffered,** and **Percent Utilization**. Like several of the performance reports, known values are displayed, while "**N/A**" displays for unknown values.

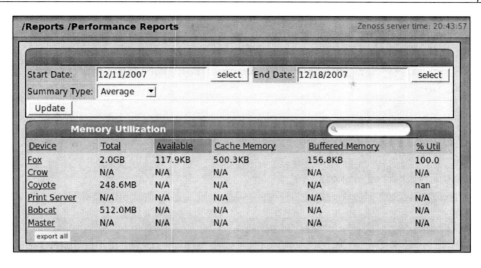

The default date range of the report includes the previous seven days, but we can specify our own **Start** and **End Dates**. We can further filter the report output by showing the maximum or Average usage statistics by choosing the appropriate option from the **Summary Type**.

Threshold Summary

To see a list of the devices that have crossed the performance threshold, we run the **Threshold Summary** Report (refer to the following screenshot) . For each **Component** listed, the report includes the **Device**, **Event Class**, and a **Count** of the threshold violations, the **Duration**, and **Percent Utilization**.

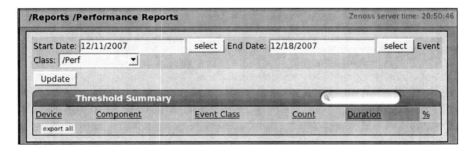

The report displays the previous seven days by default, but we can specify custom **Start** and **End Dates**. The default **Class** is **/Perf**, which includes all the performance class events; however, we can limit the report to the following event sub-classes: /Perf/CPU, /Perf/Memory, /Perf/Filesystem, /Perf/Interface, /Perf/Snmp, and /Perf/XmlRpc.

User Reports

The User Reports organizer includes user-centric reports. We'll review the Notification Schedules report.

Notification Schedules

The **Notification Schedules** Report (see the next screen capture) displays each alerting rule by name, with the assigned user. The other fields on the report include alert delays, active status, alert **Duration**, and **Next Active** window. Each alert includes two rows on the report, and on the second row, we see the actual alert criteria.

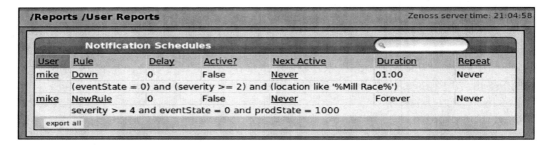

Summary

Now that we have wrapped up our discussion on Zenoss reporting, we have all the tools necessary to manage our device inventory, including discovery, monitoring, and event management. In Chapter 9, we will turn our attention to administering the Zenoss system. We'll manage users, alerts, and perform general Zenoss maintenance.

9
Settings and Administration

Monitoring our IT resources means little unless we alert our staff to problems, so we'll spend the first part of this chapter reviewing alerting rules and user management. Alerting rules are tied to users, and we need alerting rules to notify our users of outages. Once we configure our alerting rules, we have a fully functioning monitoring environment.

After alerting rules, we will cover many of the system settings that control the Zenoss UI, notification protocols, and daemons. No administration discussion would be complete without talking about backups and updates, so we'll end the chapter by talking about common Zenoss tasks including backups and updates.

Alerting Rules

To finish setting up our monitoring environment, we need to add users to Zenoss and configure alerting rules so that events trigger an action. Actions can be notifications via email or pager, or we can run shell commands based on our alerting rules.

User Management

We should set up a user name for each person who will be using Zenoss, and all the users should log in using their user account, not as the admin user. Individual users can be granted the same privileges as the admin account; however, working as the non-admin user has several benefits:

- Changes to settings are tracked via user name
- Custom alerting rules can be defined per user
- Access can be restricted per user

Let's add a new user:

1. Select **Settings** from the navigation panel.
2. Select the **Users** tab.
3. From the **Users** table menu, select Add New User.
4. Enter the User Name and Email address in the Add User dialog box.
5. Click OK to create the user account.

The new user name is added to the list of users (see following screenshot) along with columns for **Email** address, **Pager**, address, and **Roles**.

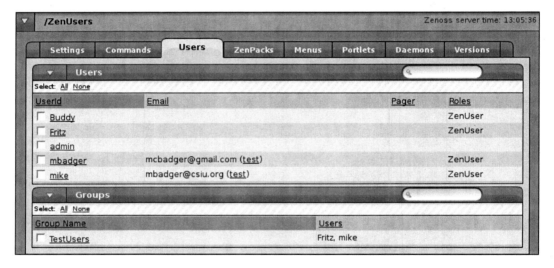

Before a new user can log in, we must specify a password. To create a password and configure the account, edit the user account by clicking on the user name from the **Users** table. The following table includes the fields we can set via the Edit Screen.

Property	Description
Password	Specify the new password in the first text field. Retype the password in the second box and click save to verify the passwords match.
Roles	Specify a user role. Available options are Manager, ZenManager, and ZenUser.
Groups	If the user is a member of a defined group, select it. Groups are defined in Settings > Users.
Email	Enter an email address if the user has to receive alerts via email.

Property	Description
Pager	Enter a pager number if the user will receive alerts via pager.
Default Page Size	Specify number of entries displayed in a grid listing. Default is 40.
Default Admin Role	Select the default role for administered objects.
Default Admin Level	This field is not currently used and is reserved for future use.
Dashboard Refresh	Enter the time in seconds that the dashboard refreshes for the user. The default is 30 seconds.
Dashboard Timeout	Enter the time in seconds before the dashboard refresh timeouts. The default is 25 seconds.
Dashboard Organizer	Select the organizer view for the Device Issues dashboard portlet. The user can change or select a new organizer via the Preferences link. Available options include: Devices Systems Groups Locations
Network Map Start Object	Specify a default network from the monitored networks to map on the Network Maps view. For example, 192.168.1.1.

We use roles to define a user's level of access to the system. The following table lists the available roles from the most to the least restrictive access.

Role	Access Privileges
ZenUser	View-only access to the system includes the Dashboard, Device List, Browse By organizers, and classes.
ZenManager	Access includes view, update, and delete. User is able to access the Management menu items and Event Console.

Administered Objects

For each user, we can assign a list of administered objects, which includes devices, systems, groups, and locations. By matching users to administered objects, we have an easy way to identify who is responsible for the object. The following screenshot shows the **Administered Objects** for a user.

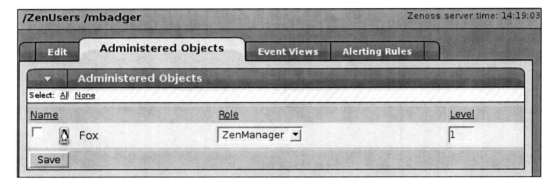

To add an object, choose the appropriate option from the **Administered Objects** page menu. If we add a device, the Add Device dialog box filters the list of devices as we type. If we add a system, group, or location, we choose the object from a drop-down list.

Each administered object has a default role that we can change. We specify the user's default admin role on each user's Edit tab.

If we click on the object name, Zenoss displays the Status page for the device, system, group, or location. Each object also has an Administration page that lists the users identified as administrators. For example, navigate to a device and select **More > Administration** from the page menu to see the list of administrators for the device.

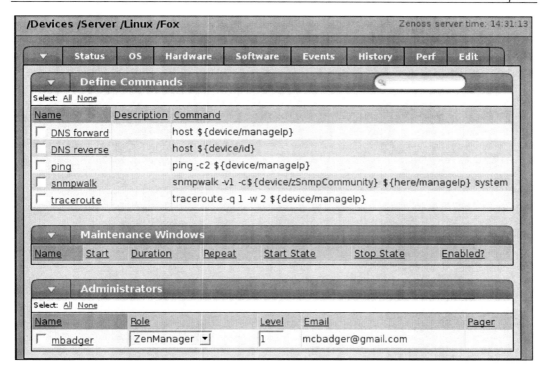

From the **Administrators** table of the object (see the previous screenshot), we see a list of users and **Roles**. Click on the user name to navigate back to the user's Edit page.

Event Views

In Chapter 7, we discussed Event Views in detail. Zenoss enables us to create custom event views per user. To define a custom event view for a user:

1. Edit the user.
2. Select the **Event Views** tab.
3. From the Event Views table menu, select Add Event View.
4. Enter a descriptive name (e.g: Events on Coyote) in the Add Event View dialog box.
5. Click OK to add the event view.

Each event view displays columns for type and event summary. By default, the newly created event view looks identical to the Event Console. Click on the name from the Event Views list to display and edit the view (see the following screen capture).

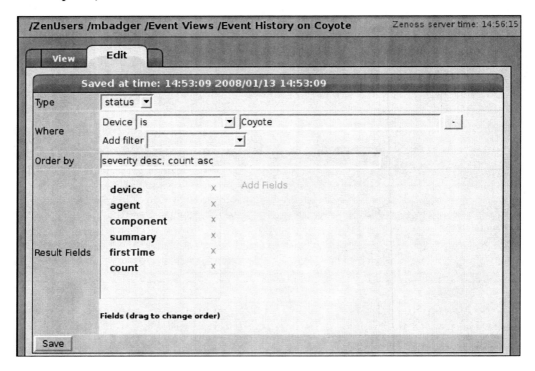

From the edit tab, we specify the following event view properties:

Property	Description
Type	Select "**status**" to display active events and "history" to display cleared events.
Where	Build the filtering rules for the event view. For example: "**Device is Coyote.**"
Order by	Specify the default sort order. Sort orders are specified in pairs by field and order. Each sort order is comma separated. For example, if we specify a sort order equal to "**severity desc, count asc**" the event view lists all the events from the most severe to the least severe. Within each severity, the view sorts by the count field in ascending order.
Result Fields	Add and remove fields to the event view.

After we edit the view, click **Save**. Then click on the **View** tab so that the view gets displayed.

Alerting Rules

We attach alerts to users or groups of users. We'll cover groups in the next section, but for now, we'll add an alerting rule at the user level. To add an alerting rule, select the **Alerting Rules** tab (see the following screenshot) while editing the user name to display the list of rules assigned to the user.

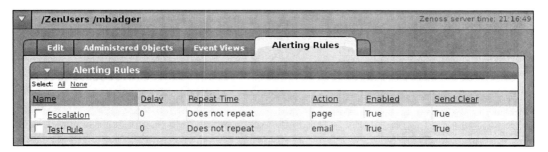

The Alerting Rules table displays a summary of each rule including columns for **Name, Delay, Repeat Time, Action, Enabled,** and **Send Clear**. To add a new alerting rule:

1. Select Add Alerting Rules from the **Alerting Rules** table menu.
2. Enter a descriptive name in the Add Alerting Rule dialog box.
3. Click OK to add the new rule.
4. Click on the name in the Alerting Rules table to edit the rule properties (see the next screenshot).
5. Configure the alert and click **Save**.

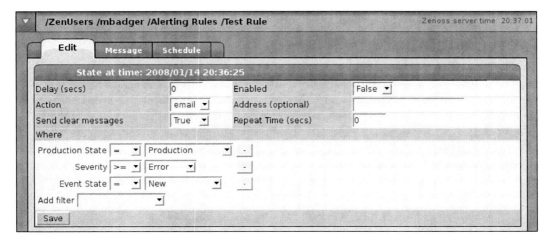

The default rule sends an email when any device in a **Production State** generates a new event with a **Severity** level equal to or greater than **Error**. Zenoss also sends an alert when the event clears. However, the alert is disabled by default.

Let's take a look at each of the Alerting Rule properties:

Property	Description
Delay (secs)	Delay sending the alert for the specified time. Default is **0**.
Enabled	Set to **True** to enable the alert. If the value is **False**, this rule does not send alerts.
Action	Choose either **email** or pager notifications.
Address (optional)	Specify any valid email address. If left blank, the email address specified for the user is used.
Send clear messages	Select **True** to send alerts when the event clears. Select **False** to suppress clear messages.
Repeat Time (secs)	Repeat the alerting rule for the specified time. Default is **0**.
Where	Select the event filter criteria. Add and remove filters as needed.

An event filter consists of three parts: an event field, a comparison operator, and a value to compare to the event field.

We add a filter by selecting the event field from the **Add Filter** drop-down list. See Appendix A for a list of fields. Next, we specify a comparison operator, such as greater-than and less-than. Then we specify a value to match against the operator. The More filters we add to a rule, the more specific our alerting rule becomes.

Alert Escalations

By using the filters on an alerting rule, we can create an alert hierarchy that notifies another user when a certain condition occurs. We can create a new rule for a second user and add a filter that specifies a count value so that if the event is not acknowledged, the user is notified. For example, if our new filter specifies a count greater than five, we define a rule that does not trigger unless an event remains unacknowledged for five consecutive times. We talked about acknowledging events as part of the event work flow in Chapter 7.

Message

While editing our alerting rule, we have the ability to customize the text of the alert message Zenoss sends. To view the Message, click on the **Message** tab.

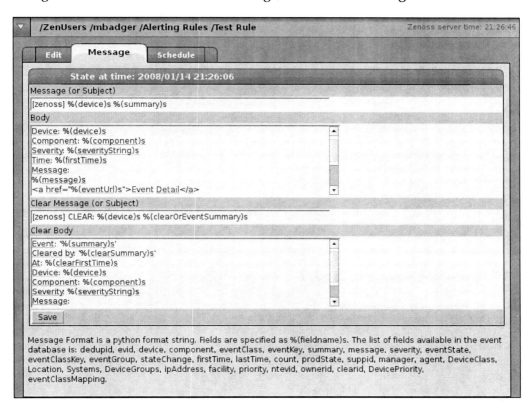

We can specify the **Subject** and the **Body** for both the down alert and the clear alert. As the text at the bottom of the **Message** tab indicates, the "**message format is a Python format string. Fields are specified as %(fieldname)s.**" (refer to the previous screenshot). All the event fields are listed for reference.

If we set the alerting rule to send a page, we can only specify a subject line for the down and clear alerts because of likely character restrictions on the pager.

Schedule

We may set a schedule for each alerting rule so that the rule sends alerts only during the specified period. From the Edit tab of an alerting rule, click on the **Schedule** tab to view the **Active Periods** table. The **Active Periods** table displays a list of schedules sorted by **Name** with columns for **Start**, **Duration**, **Repeat**, and **Enabled**, as shown in the next screen capture.

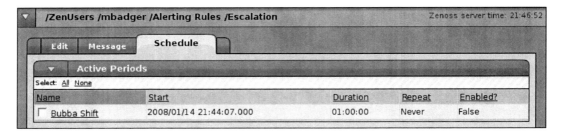

To add a schedule, select Add Rule Window from the Active Periods table menu. Enter a descriptive name when prompted. Click OK to add the new schedule to the Active Periods table. Click on the name to display the active period's Status page.

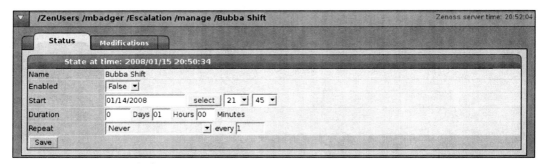

On the Status page for the active period, we define the time of day when the alerting schedule is active (see the previous screenshot). The following table lists the available settings.

Property	Description
Enabled	Set to True to enable the alerting rule during the specified time and duration.
Start	Specify the start date, hour, and minute. The hours are specified in 24-hour time.
Duration	Enter the **Days**, **Hours**, and **Minutes** to keep the alerting rule active after it starts.

Property	Description
Repeat	Select the interval and frequency. Available intervals are: • **Never** • **Daily** • **Every weekday** • **Weekly** • **Monthly** • **First Sunday of the month** Enter a frequency to repeat the selected interval.

We may add as many active periods to an alerting rule as we need to accommodate each user's work schedule.

Groups

We've just learnt how to define alerting rules on a per user basis, but if we have more than two or three users, we need a better way to handle our alerting rules. Fortunately, Zenoss provides groups, and the same alerting rule concepts that apply to users apply to groups.

We start by adding a new group to the Groups table of the Users tab in the Settings page. Next, we assign users to the group in the following way:

1. Select the group name.

2. Select **Add Users** from the **Group** table menu.

3. Choose the user names (*ctrl + click* to select multiple) from the **Add Users To Group** dialog box (refer to the following screenshot).

4. Select the **Group** name from the **Add Users to Group** dialog box.

5. Click **OK** to assign the users to the group.

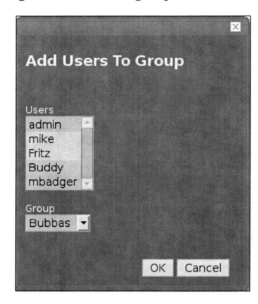

Now that we have a newly created group with users assigned, click on the group name to display the group's Edit tab. From the Edit tab, we can add and remove users from our group. On the Administered Objects tab, we identify the relationship a device, system, group, or location has to a group.

To begin adding alerting rules for the group, select the Alerting Rules tab and follow the steps outlined in the previous section for individual users.

System Settings

In addition to the Simple Mail Transport Protocol (SMTP) and Simple Network Paging Protocol (SNPP) host configuration, the Settings page displays other site configurations, such as state and priority conversions. Before Zenoss can send alerts, we need to configure the SMTP and SNPP hosts' information, depending on which notification method we use for our alerting rules. To access the Settings, click on **Settings** from the navigation panel (refer to the next screenshot).

The following table lists the available settings.

Property	Description
SMTP Host	The address of the SMTP server.
SMTP Port	The SMTP port. The default is **25**.
SMTP Username	If the SMTP server requires authentication to send mail, specify the user name to send the mail. Zenoss sends the SMTP user name and password when needed.
SMTP Password	Specify the password for the SMTP user name.
From Address for Emails	Alerts will come from the specified email address.
Use TLS?	If the SMTP host uses Transport Layer Security, check this box.
SNPP Host	Specify the Simple Network Paging Protocol host.
SNPP Port	Specify the SNPP Port number. Default is **444**.
Dashboard Production State Threshold	The dashboard displays devices with a threshold equal to or greater than the specified value. Default is **1000**.
Dashboard Priority Threshold	The dashboard displays devices with a priority equal to or greater than the specified value. Default is **2**.
State Conversions	In descending order, Zenoss includes the following device states by default: • **Production: 1000** • **Pre-Production: 500** • **Test: 400** • **Maintenance: 300** • **Decommissioned: -1** Some places within Zenoss use the text description while other places use the numeric state.
Priority Conversions	In descending order, Zenoss uses the following device priorities: • **Highest: 5** • **High: 4** • **Normal: 3** • **Low: 2** • **Lowest: 1** • **Trivial: 0** Some places within Zenoss use the text description while other places use the numeric priority.

Property	Description
Administrative Roles	Create user-defined roles. Not currently used in Zenoss Core for event processing.
Google Maps API Key	Enter the Google Maps API key to display the map on the Locations dashboard portlet.

We can add as many states, priorities, and **Administrative Roles** as we want. For example, we could assign a group of devices to a custom state and use the state to build custom event and alerting rules.

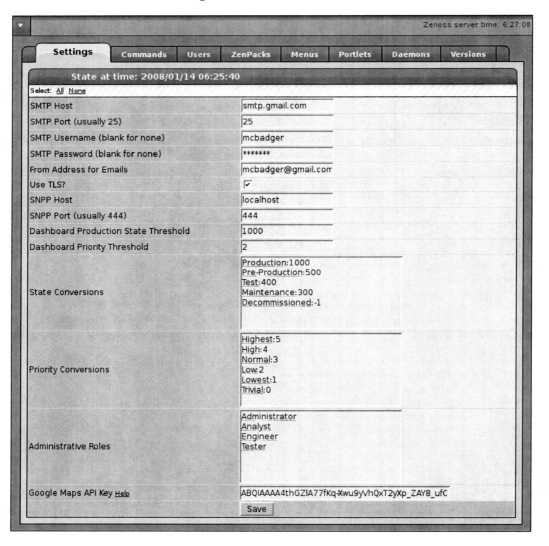

Commands

By combining shell commands and TALES expressions, we can run commands against our devices from within the Zenoss web portal. Zenoss includes the following commands by default: host, **ping**, **snmpwalk**, and **traceroute**. To see the complete syntax of these commands, navigate to **Settings > Commands**.

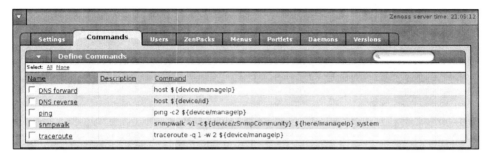

Let's examine the `ping` command. The actual command Zenoss executes against the device is **ping -c2 ${device/manageIp}**. The first half of the command construction (`ping -c2`) is a **ping** command that sends no more than two ping requests. The second half of the command (`${device/manageIp}` is a TALES expression. The `manageIp` variable provides the IP address of the current device. A list of TALES expressions can be found in Appendix B .

We run commands from a device's status page, a device class, systems organizer, group organizer, or location. For example, if we want to ping a single device, edit the device and select **Run Commands > Ping** from the page menu. If we want to ping all Linux servers, navigate to the /Server/Linux class and run the ping command from the page menu. The output displays in a new window (refer to the next screenshot).

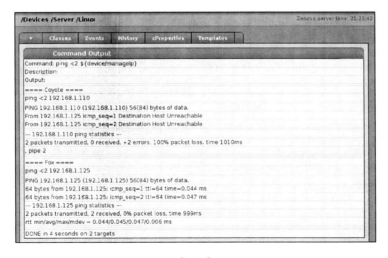

The commands are primarily a troubleshooting tool. We will walk through the process of adding a new nmap command. We use nmap to determine open ports and available services on a machine. From the Commands tab:

1. Select Add User Command from the Commands table menu.

2. Enter a descriptive name (e.g.: nmap) in the Add User Command dialog box.

3. Click OK to add the command and display the command properties.

4. Type a short explanation in the Description field: "Display interesting ports on a device".

5. Enter the following in the Command field: `nmap -v ${device/manageIp}`.

6. Click Save.

Now, we will test our command on a device to make sure it does what we expect.

Menus

You don't like the menu order on a page? The Menus tab enables us to change how the menus display within Zenoss. When we navigate to **Settings > Menus**, the Menus tab displays a Menu ID selection that corresponds to various menu trees throughout the Zenoss portal. Select the Menu ID to display the individual menu items associated with the Menu ID. Each menu item has an associated Ordering, **Description**, and **Action**. The **Description** is the text that displays when we access the menu. The **Action** displays the object which the menu calls. Ordering defines the sequence which the menus display.

In order to add a menu, we need to know the Menu Item, **Description**, and **Action** values.

As an example, we will remove a menu item and then replace it. Let's remove the Delete Device option from the Manage menu.:

1. Select **Manage** from the **Menu ID** drop down list.

2. Record the Ordering, **Menu Item, Description**, and **Action** values for deleteDevice.

3. Select the deleteDevice menu item from the **Menu** table.

4. Select **Delete Menu Items** from the **Menu** table (refer to the following screen capture). The individual menus display in the **Menu** table.

5. Click **OK** to confirm the delete.

To verify our action, we can navigate to the device's status page. From the page menu, select More. Note that Delete Device is no longer an option.

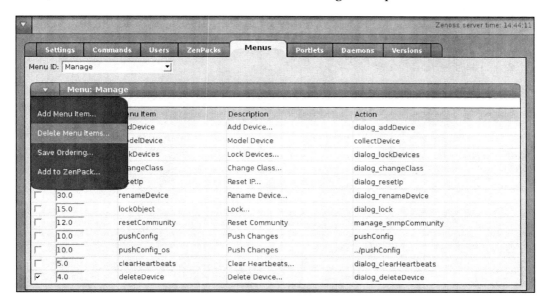

Let's add the Delete Device Menu back:

1. Select **Manage** from the Menu ID drop-down list.
2. Select **Add Menu Item** from the table menu.
3. In the **Add Menu Item** dialog box, enter the following values:
   ◦ ID: deleteDevice
   ◦ Description: Delete Devices...
   ◦ Action: dialog_deleteDevice
   ◦ Ordering: 4.0
4. Click OK to add the menu.

When we view the the Manage menu for a device, we can select **Delete Device**.

Portlets Permission

We can restrict which users see which dashboard portlets by setting permissions on the **Portlets** tab in Settings. We can choose from three levels (refer to the following screen capture):

- **Users with Manage DMD permission**
- **Users with View permission**
- **Users with ZenCommon permission**

The three permission levels correspond to the three Zenoss roles: Manager, ZenManager, and ZenUser. Functionally speaking, however, the Users with Manage DMD and Users with ZenCommon permissions apply equally to users in the Manager and ZenManager roles (as of Zenoss Core 2.1.2).

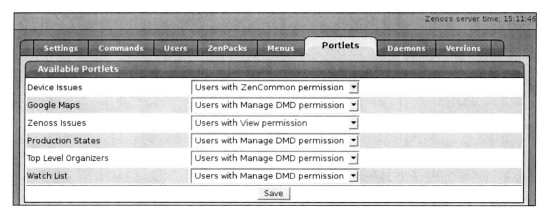

If we want to restrict users within the ZenUsers role from seeing a dashboard portlet, assign the portlet **Users with Manage DMD permission**. Users who are members of either the Manager or ZenManager role will be able to see all the device portlets regardless of the set permission.

Don't forget to Save changes.

Zenoss Daemons

A daemon is a process that runs in the background on Unix systems and is comparable to what Windows calls a service. To see a list of Zenoss daemons, navigate to **Settings** > **Daemons** for each daemon, we see the process ID (**PID**), **Log File**, **Configuration**, **State**, and **Actions**, as shown in the following screen capture.

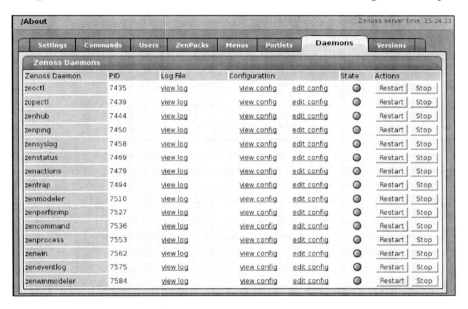

We've been working with these daemons from the very beginning through our actions within the Zenoss UI. As we look over the list of daemons, we can speculate what some of these processes are responsible for. For example, **zensyslog** processes syslogs, **zenmodeler** creates the model of our devices based on the plug-ins defined for each device, and **zenping** monitors device availability each minute.

We usually turn to the Daemons tab when we're curious or troubleshooting. Click on the view log link to display the log file for each daemon. We find the raw logs in the $ZENHOME/log directory.

If we want to override the default daemon behavior, we can edit the configuration by clicking on the **edit config** link, and naturally, the **view config** link displays the current configuration. To view the available options for each daemon, open a command line environment and type the name of the daemon followed by the word help. To see zenmodeler's options, we type:

```
zenmodeler help
```

The output is as shown in the following figure.

```
File  Edit  View  Terminal  Tabs  Help
mike@fox:/usr/local/zenoss/log$ zenmodeler help
usage: zenmodeler.py [options]

options:
  --version             show program's version number and exit
  -h, --help            show this help message and exit
  -v LOGSEVERITY, --logseverity=LOGSEVERITY
                        Logging severity threshold
  --logpath=LOGPATH     override default logging path
  -C CONFIGFILE, --configfile=CONFIGFILE
                        config file must define all params (see man)
  --uid=UID             user to become when running default:zenoss
  -c, --cycle           Cycle continuously on cycleInterval from zope
  -D, --daemon          Become a unix daemon
  --weblog              output log info in html table format
  --host=HOST           hostname of zeo server
  --port=PORT           port of zeo server
  -R DATAROOT, --dataroot=DATAROOT
```

The syntax we use to enter command parameters and values via the web interface varies from the way we specify options on the command line. In our example, we will increase zenmodeler's logging level from the default INFO to a more verbose DEBUG. On the command line, we use the following command as the Zenoss User:

```
zenmodeler restart --logseverity=4
```

If we use the edit config link via the Daemons tab, we specify the parameters and values via a space delineated list. See the following screenshot.

Don't forget to save the configuration. Then click the restart button for the zenmodeler daemon to pass the new configuration to the daemon. To view the results of our change, click on the view log link and scroll to the bottom. We see the results of our action and our logs now show debugging messages.

Each of the daemon configuration files can be found in the $ZENHOME/etc directory, and we can edit them with a text editor if we choose to.

Maintenance Windows

If we plan to take a device out of service for maintenance or other scheduled down time, we can set up a maintenance window so that Zenoss does not alert us of a problem when our scheduled maintenance starts. We define maintenance windows via the Administration properties of devices, device classes, systems, groups, or locations. We'll walk through a sample maintenance window for our web server Coyote:

1. Click the device from the Device List to display the device's status page.
2. From the page menu, select **More** > **Administration**.
3. From the **Maintenance Windows** table menu, select Add Maint Window.
4. In the Add Maintenance Window dialog box, enter a descriptive name: (e.g.: Test Window).
5. Click OK to add the maintenance window.

Our new Test Window rule is displayed in the Maintenance Windows table, but we still need to configure and enable the rule. Click on the name to edit the rule properties (see the following screenshot).

The following table outlines the available maintenance window properties.

Property	Description
Enabled	Select true to activate the Maintenance window. Default is **False**.
Start	Enter the start date and time.
Duration	Specify the duration in **Days**, **Hours**, and **Minutes**.
Repeat	Select the interval to repeat the maintenance window. Available intervals are: • **Never** • Daily • Every weekday • Weekly • Monthly • First Sunday of the month
Start Production State	Specify the production state to move the devices into, once the maintenance window starts. Default is **Maintenance**.
Stop Production State	Specify the production state for the device after the maintenance window ends. The default selection is **Original**.

By setting the production state to **Maintenance**, Zenoss continues to monitor the device; however, it will not send any alerts.

Add MIBs

We haven't talked about Management Information Database's files since Chapter 3, but at some point, we may need an MIB that Zenoss does not provide. If we see OID numbers (for example, .1.3.6.1.4.1.311.1.1.3.1.3) in our events, then that's a good sign which indicates that we need to update our MIBs. To find an MIB and its dependencies, we can search the following resources:

- Vendor's support site
- Web search for the OID
- MIB search sites, such as `http://www.mibsearch.com`

We will use the `MSFT-MIB.mib` file to demonstrate how to register a MIB with Zenoss. First, copy the `MSFT-MIB.mib` to `$ZENHOME/share/mibs/site/`. Second, run the following command as the Zenoss user:

```
zenmib run
```

If the command is successful, we will see the following output in our command output:

```
INFO:zen.zenmib:Loaded mib MSFT-MIB
```

We can see the result of our action by logging into the Zenoss UI and selecting MIBs from the navigation panel. Our newly registered MIB is displayed in the table along with the number of nodes mapped by the MIB. Click on the name to display the contents of the MIB file. Refer to the following screen capture which shows the OID mappings of an imported MIB file.

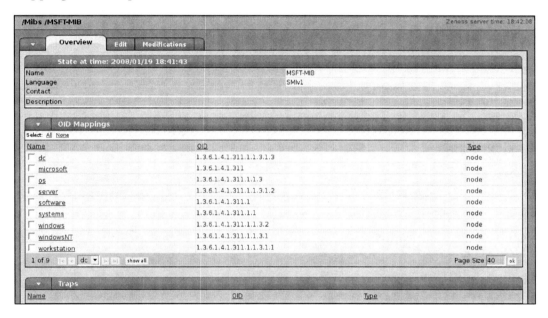

By looking at the contents of the MIB, we can see the human friendly names each node (OID) maps to.

Back Up and Restore

Zenoss provides two command line utilities that enable us to back up and restore key pieces of our Zenoss configuration. The zenbackup command backs up the following components:

- MySQL events
- Zope database
- `$ZENHOME/etc`
- Performance data

To create the backup, run the following commands as the zenoss user:

```
zenoss stop
zenbackup
zenoss start
```

We stop the Zenoss service before running the backup command and we start Zenoss after the backup completes. To see a list of available options, run `zenbackup` with the `--help` option.

The `zenbackup` command creates a zipped file in the `$ZENHOME/backups` directory. An example backup file would be named `zenbackup_20080119.tgz`, which keeps the file names unique by using the date the backup is created.

In order to restore the backup file, we need to know the backup file name and the events database password. If our system uses a non-Zenoss default events database name and credentials, then we need to specify that information in our `zenrestore` command. To see a list of all the available options, append the `--help` option to the `zenrestore` command. To restore our backup file, run the following commands as the Zenoss user:

```
zenoss stop
zenrestore --file=$ZENHOME/backups/zenbackup_20080119.tgz --dbpass=mypass
zenoss start
```

Of course, we will substitute the file name and database password with the ones that match our individual environments.

Automate Backups

We can schedule regular backups with cron, a Unix-based daemon. In our example, we'll create a script in the `/home/zenoss/bin` directory and schedule it to run via crontab, which is a utility that allows individual users to schedule recurring tasks.

As the Zenoss user, save the following bash script as `zenoss_daily` to `/home/zenoss/bin/`:

```
#!/bin/bash

# This script contains a short list of Zenoss commands that
# we want to run daily via cron.

#Setup Zenoss environment
export ZENHOME=/usr/local/zenoss
export PYTHONPATH=$ZENHOME/lib/python
```

```
export PATH=$ZENHOME/bin:$PATH

# Back up Zenoss and capture the verbose stdout to a log
zenbackup -v > $HOME\zenoss_daily.log

# end script
```

After we save the zenoss_daily script, we need to make it executable. As the Zenoss user, run the following command:

chmod +x $HOME/bin/zenoss_daily

Next, we need to schedule our script to run at a regular interval via the Zenoss users crontab entry.

In order for the Zenoss user to use crontab, the user name "zenoss" must either appear in the /etc/cron.allow file or must not appear in the /etc/cron.deny file depending on the system cofiguration. As an example, we'll add "zenoss" to /etc/cron.allow by adding a new line with the user name "zenoss" on it. If /etc/cron.allow does not exist, we can create it as root using our favorite text editor.

When we define a crontab entry, we define the minute, hour, day of the month, month, or day of the week followed by the command to run. The following table shows valid values for each time, day, and date field.

Time Intervals (Listed in the order they appear in crontab)	Valid Values
Minute	0 - 59
Hour	0 – 23
Day of Month	1 – 31
Month	1 – 12 (January = 1)
Day of Week	0 - 6 (Sunday = 0)

Let's set our zenoss_daily script to run at 11:30 PM daily. As the zenoss user, invoke the crontab editor with the following command:

crontab-e

Make the following entry into the crontab editor and save it:

```
30 23 * * * /home/zenoss/bin/zenoss_daily
```

In this example, we're not specifying a day of the month, month, or day of the week, so we use an asterisk (*) for those fields. To verify that our command runs each day, check $ZENHOME/backups for a backup file for each day. We can also review the /home/zenoss/zenoss_daily.log file that we use to capture the output of the zenbackup command.

Update Zenoss Core

Zenoss releases major versions that add features and follows up with maintenance releases. For example, Zenoss 2.1 is a feature release and primarily adds functionality, while Zenoss 2.1.2 represents a maintenance release that increases stability.

Zenoss also outputs sprint releases every 30 days. Sprint gives out a regular release schedule that allows Zenoss and the community to preview and test features that are in progress and scheduled for upcoming stable releases. The features are often functional but incomplete.

Part of the update process implies that we know about the software we have installed right now. To view information about the current Zenoss installation, we navigate to **Settings > Versions** (see the following screen capture).

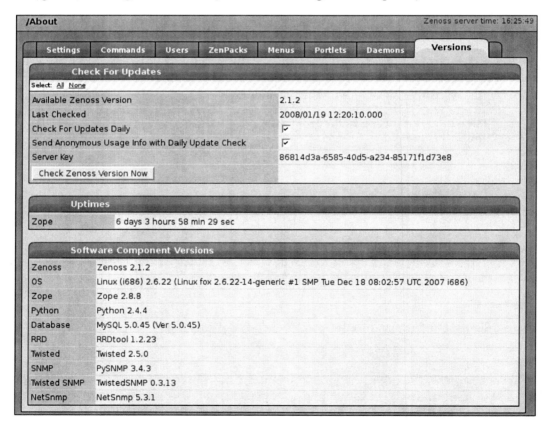

The **Versions** tab shows us version information about Zenoss, its core components, and the host operating system. In the **Check For Updates** table, we click the **Check Zenoss Version Now** button to get the latest version number, which is then reported as the Available Zenoss Version. If that number is greater than the installed Zenoss version listed in the **Software Component Versions** table, we have an upgrade available.

Zenoss does not upgrade automatically. We need to download the update from `http://www.zenoss.com/download/`. The update procedure depends on whether or not we are using an RPM, source, or virtual appliance install.

Prior to updating Zenoss, we should make sure that we back up our monitoring data with zenbackup as discussed in the Back up and Restore section. As an extra safeguard, we can backup the entire $ZENHOME directory prior to updating in case the entire update process somehow goes awry.

RPM Update

Before we install the new RPM, we stop the Zenoss daemons with the following command as the Zenoss user:

```
zenoss stop
```

Next, install the downloaded RPM with the following command as root:

```
rpm -Uvh zenoss-<version #>.rpm
```

Replace the `<version #>` with the correct name of the downloaded file.

After the installation completes, start Zenoss with the following command as the Zenoss user:

```
zenoss start
```

Log in to the Zenoss UI as before.

Source Update

To update the source install, unpack the current source and run the install script located in the top level of the source directory as the Zenoss user:

```
./install.sh
```

The installer prompts us with two questions. The installer asks us to enter the password for the Zenoss admin user. It also asks us if we want to keep our existing database. The default answer is yes. If we answer no, our existing device and event database will be wiped out and we'll have to start from scratch. The expected answer here is Y for yes.

After Zenoss builds and installs the update, the install script prompts us to update the permissions on zensocket. As root, run the following commands:

```
chown root:zenoss /usr/local/zenoss/bin/zensocket
chmod 04750 /usr/local/zenoss/bin/zensocket
```

Finally, restart the Zenoss daemons by running the following command as the Zenoss user:

```
zenoss start
```

Log in to the Zenoss portal as before.

Virtual Appliance Update

Virtual appliance users can update to the next version of Zenoss by using the package manager conary. Log in to the Zenoss virtual image as the Zenoss user and stop Zenoss:

```
zenoss stop
```

As root, update Zenoss with the command:

```
conary update zenoss --resolve
```

If conary complains about unresolvable python dependencies, then run the following commands:

```
conary update python --resolve
conary update zenoss --zenoss
```

To finish the update, restart Zenoss as the Zenoss user:

```
zenoss start
```

Log in to Zenoss as usual.

Summary

Now that we have concluded our Zenoss administration discussion, we have all the tools to implement and maintain a highly customizable monitoring solution. In the previous chapters, we monitored devices and generated events, and in this chapter we have completed our monitoring solution by turning events into alerts. As we found out, there's more to administering Zenoss than defining alerting rules and user management. We looked at the various ways to control system-wide monitoring properties through daemons, system settings, and custom user commands. Our chapter concluded by updating Zenoss Core to the latest version after we learnt how to back up and restore.

In the next chapter, we'll take a look at extending Zenoss' functionality through its ZenPack architecture, as well as some advanced command line usage.

10
Extend Zenoss

In this chapter, we take advantage of some of the Zenoss Core's advanced features to extend our monitoring and reporting capabilities. Specifically, we will install and create ZenPacks, configure external plug-ins, and turn emails into events.

To accomplish some of our tasks, we move away from the comforts of the graphical user interface and spend some time working with several Zenoss commands from the command line interface.

ZenPacks

ZenPacks provide an architecture that allows us to customize Zenoss and share those customizations between installations or with the community at large. ZenPack authors can choose to create their ZenPacks from the web interface or program Zenpacks. From the web interface, we package changes to the following components: Event and Device classes, services, processes, reports, MIBs, menus, commands, and performance templates. If we want to add a new daemon or modify the web interface, then we need to write the ZenPack programmatically.

We'll use the web interface to accomplish the tasks that most administrators will need. We'll walk through an example that packages several new user commands into a ZenPack. For the programmers among us, Zenoss provides an example HelloWorldZenPack on the Zenoss ZenPack Project Site at `http://www.zenoss.com/community/projects/zenpacks/`.

Before we jump into creating a ZenPack on our own, let's take a look at the ZenPacks currently available from Zenoss. The ZenPack Project Site organizes the packages into three categories: Community, Core, and Enterprise.

The community ZenPacks are created and shared by Zenoss community members. They are available as-is. The Core ZenPacks are created and distributed by Zenoss for all to use. The Enterprise ZenPacks are reserved for customers who purchased Zenoss Enterprise and are not available to Zenoss Core users.

Install

Incorporating a ZenPack into our Zenoss system includes three steps:

1. Download the ZenPack from the the Zenoss ZenPack Project Site.
2. Install the ZenPack.
3. Configure the devices to use the ZenPack.

Let's demonstrate the process with the HttpMonitor ZenPack, which monitors the status and response time of a website using the Nagios plug-in check_http.

Monitor Websites with HttpMonitor

Hopefully, the ZenPacks we install have appropriate documentation that tells us how to take advantage of the new functionality. In the case of the HttpMonitor ZenPack, we know by reading the Zenoss documentation that the ZenPack adds the /Status/Web event class and the HttpMonitor data source, which allows us to generate performance graphs.

In our example, the real work begins after we install the ZenPack. We add the website to be monitored as a device and create a custom performance template that we will use to add data sources and graphs.

Let's begin by installing the HttpMonitor ZenPack:

1. Download the HttpMonitor package from the Zenoss ZenPack Project Site, but do not unzip the file.
2. Navigate to **Settings > ZenPacks** in Zenoss.
3. From the Loaded ZenPacks table menu, select **Install ZenPack**.
4. Browse for and select the ZenPack we downloaded.
5. Click **OK** to install the ZenPack.

After the ZenPack installs, Zenoss displays the results of the ZenPack installation in the browser window, as shown in the following screen capture.

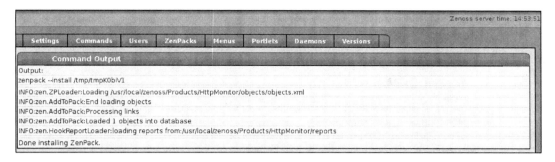

If we want to monitor only one website, we could create a custom performance template at the device level, but in our example, we assume that we want to monitor several URLs. Therefore, we'll use Zenoss' hierarchy and create a new /Web device class to organize our websites.

The following sequence of steps adds the web domain in the /Web device class and creates a custom performance template that we will configure. This process incorporates many of the concepts we've used throughout the book to manage our devices. It's now a good time to review the performance template section in Chapter 6.

Let's monitor badgerfiles.com or any other website:

1. Create the /Web device class.
2. Add a new device with the following properties:
   - Device Name: badgerfiles.com
   - Device Class Path: /Web
   - Discovery Protocol: None
3. Select **badgerfiles.com** from the Device List.
4. From the device's page menu, select **More > Templates**.
5. Click Create Local Copy for the Device performance template.
6. Edit the device template and make the following changes:
   - Name: HttpMonitor
   - Description: Monitor the status and performance of URLs.
   - Remove the sysUpTime Data Source.

7. From the Data Sources menu, select Add Data Source.

8. In the Add a new Data Source dialog box:

    • Enter a descriptive name in the ID field (e.g.: pageLoad)

    • Type HttpMonitor

9. Click OK to add the data source and display its properties
    (see the following screenshot).

At this point, our /Web device class does not have any performance templates
associated with it because we renamed the local copy of the device template, which
means our new device does not have a performance template either. We will bind
the template to the /Web class in a few minutes. For now, we should use the bread
crumb navigation to move up and down the performance template hierarchy
to make changes to the HttpMonitor template. We can also edit the template by
navigating to Devices > Templates.

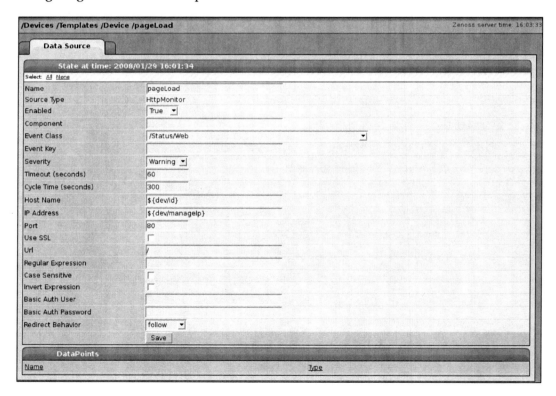

When we set the Data **Source Type** to **HttpMonitor**, we got a custom set of data source properties that correspond to the check_http command found in $ZENHOME/libexec. To see an explanation of the available options, we can run the following command from the command line:

```
$ZENHOME/libexec/check_http -help
```

We can configure our data source in a way that meets our individual needs. For example, we may want to change the **Severity** to Error or **Use SSL**. Perhaps our site requires authentication. All these options, and more are available.

After we save the data source properties, two new data points display in the Data Points table: Size and time. We'll use these data points to create a new graph:

1. Navigate back to the HttpMonitor Performance Template.
2. From the Graph Definitions table menu, select Add Graph.
3. In the Add Graph dialog, enter a descriptive name (e.g.: Website Performance) in the ID field.
4. Click OK to add the graph and display the Graph Definition properties.
5. From the Graph Points table menu, select Add Data Point.
6. In the **Add GraphPoint** dialog box, select the **pageLoad_size** or **pageLoad_time Data Points** depending on whether we want to see the size or time (see the next screenshot).
7. Click **OK** to add the graph points.

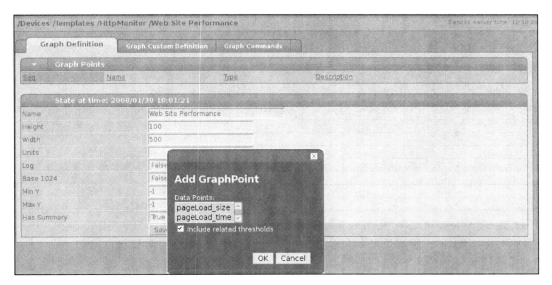

After we add the graph points, we can configure the graph definition properties as needed. Save any changes and navigate back to to the HttpMonitor Performance Template page. If we want to see graphs for both size and time values, use the same process to create a second graph.

In our final step, we need to bind the HttpMonitor performance template to the /Web device class:

1. From the navigation menu, select Devices, then /Web.

2. Select the Template tab to display a list of available performance templates.

3. From the Available Performance Templates table menu, select Bind Templates.

4. From the **Bind Performance Templates** dialog box, select **HttpMonitor** (refer to the next screen capture).

5. Click **OK** to bind the template.

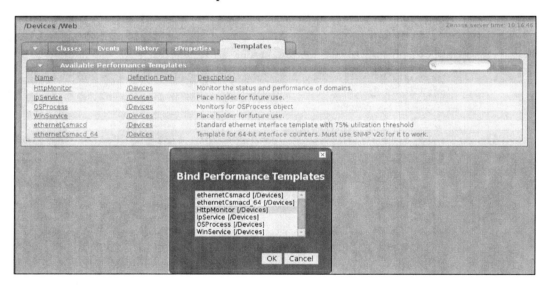

When we bind the template to the device class, all the devices in the class inherit the template's properties.

Now, we test our work. Select badgerfiles.com from the Device List and select the Perf tab. If we see the **Web Site Performance** graph as shown in the following screenshot, we are successful.

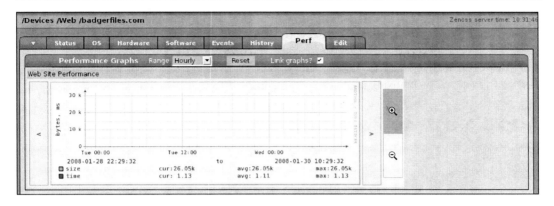

The HttpMonitor ZenPack required us to manually configure several components that could easily be incorporated into the ZenPack. For example, the ZenPack could reduce our configuration steps by including the /Web device class and the HttpMonitor performance template. The good news is that we now have access to the ZenPack, so we can add and remove objects as we deem necessary.

In our next ZenPack example, we'll go through the steps to create a new ZenPack.

Create

With the basics of installing a ZenPack behind us, we can try our hand at creating a new ZenPack that includes several custom user commands. In Chapter 9, we added the nmap command. We'll use that command as the first component in our ZenPack. To create a ZenPack, we perform the following steps: Customize Zenoss, add the customizations to a ZenPack, and export the ZenPack for deployment.

Our first step is to create the User_Commands ZenPack organizer:

1. From the navigation window, select **Settings > ZenPacks**.
2. From the Loaded ZenPacks table menu, select Create a ZenPack.
3. In the Create a new ZenPack dialog box, enter descriptive values for the ID, Author, Organization, and Version text boxes.
4. Click OK to add the ZenPack.

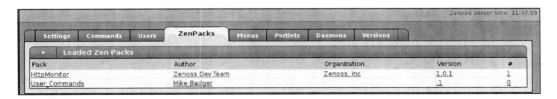

We note that our list of Loaded ZenPacks includes two items (see the preceding screenshot): The **HttpMonitor** ZenPack we installed and our new **User_Commands** ZenPack. The **Loaded ZenPacks** menu summarizes the information about the ZenPack, and it matches the values we entered in the Create a ZenPack dialog box. The last column in the table provides the **number** of objects in the ZenPack.

Add Objects to ZenPack

At the moment, we have an empty ZenPack organizer, so let's add some commands:

1. Select **Settings > Commands**.
2. Select the commands to add to the **User_Command** ZenPack.
3. From the Define Commands table menu, select **Add to ZenPack**.
4. Choose the **User_Commands** in the **Add to ZenPack** dialog box (see the next screen capture).
5. Click **Add** to add the commands.

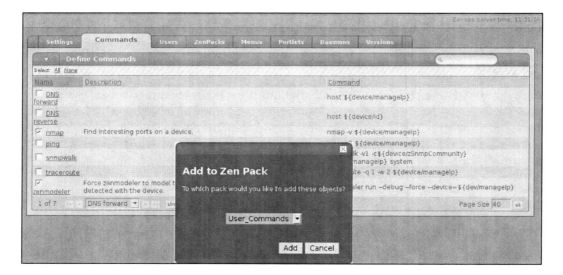

To check our work, we may navigate back to the ZenPacks tab in Settings. Now, the number of objects should change to update the number of commands we just added to the User_Commands ZenPack. Edit the User_Command ZenPack to display the **Detail** tab.

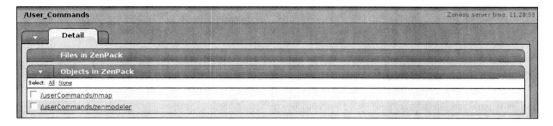

The **Detail** tab contains two tables: **Files in ZenPack** and **Objects in ZenPack**. In our example, each command we add shows up in the **Objects in ZenPack** table.

We can add as many objects to the ZenPack as needed.

Export ZenPack

Before we can contribute our ZenPack to the Zenoss community, we need to export it:

1. From the User_Commands Detail page menu, select **Export ZenPack**.
2. Choose an export option (refer to the following screen capture):
    - **Export to $ZENHOME/exports**
    - **Export to $ZENHOME/exports and download**
3. Click **OK** to export the ZenPack.

If we choose the **Export to $ZENHOME/exports and download** option, a new file is created in the exports directory of our Zenoss installation, and we are prompted to download the file via our web browser.

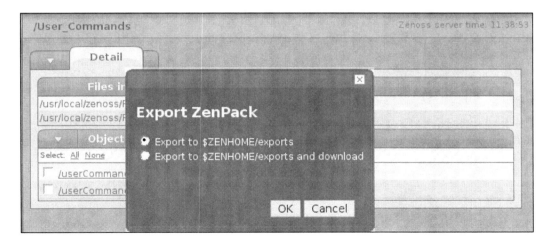

After the export process completes, make a note of the changes in the Detail tab. The Files in ZenPack table now lists the individual files that make up the ZenPack.

As a result of the export, we end up with a `User_Commands.zip` file that we can distribute among our individual Zenoss installations or to the community. Starting with Zenoss 2.2, ZenPacks will be packaged in the Python egg format, which means our file will be named `User_Commands.egg`. To install our new ZenPack, we follow the installation steps outlined in the previous section.

If at any time we wish to add objects to an existing process, we simply add the object to the applicable ZenPack. Export the ZenPack and it's ready for distribution.

Contribute ZenPacks

Zenoss does not provide an automated upload feature for community ZenPacks. If we would like to make our ZenPack available for the larger community, send an email to `community@zenoss.com`.

Plug-ins

Plug-ins allow us to gather information about our devices and services. Nagios and Cacti are two popular open-source monitoring projects and include plug-ins that support a wide range of monitoring tasks. Zenoss incorporates a plug-in framework that allows us to install Nagios and Cacti plug-ins without modification to extend the core functionality. Zenoss includes the official Nagios plug-ins in the `$ZENHOME/libexec/` directory, though we can download additional plug-ins as needed. As we demonstrated with the HttpMonitor ZenPack example, ZenPacks can include plug-ins.

In this section, we'll demonstrate how to use a plug-in with Zenoss by using the included Nagios check_procs plug-in to monitor for processes that exceed a defined CPU utilization.

Test The Plug-in

The plugi-ns are command line programs that we can run outside of Zenoss, and each plug-in has unique options we need to set in order to return the information we want to monitor. To see the command syntax, we append `--help` to the command. To see the `check_procs` usage syntax, run the command:

```
$ZENHOME/libexec/check_procs --help
```

We see the following help print to the screen:

```
Usage:check_procs -w <range> -c <range> [-m metric] [-s state] [-p ppid]
  [-u user] [-r rss] [-z vsz] [-P %cpu] [-a argument-array]
  [-C command] [-t timeout] [-v]
```

The check_procs help file is actually more verbose and explains the options in more detail. However, in the interest of space, we include only the summary help lines. We'll use check_procs to monitor the processes that have a CPU usage of over 20%, but the plug-in also monitors state, resident set memory size, virtual memory size, CPU percentage, and elapsed time.

The following example commands set a warning and a critical threshold for percent CPU usage. Each example includes a sample output to illustrate the command. As the Zenoss user, run the following commands:

```
$ZENHOME/libexec/check_procs -w 20 -c 30 --metric=CPU
CPU OK: 163 processes
$ZENHOME/libexec/check_procs -w 01 -c 30 --metric=CPU
CPU WARNING: 1 warn out of 163 processes
$ZENHOME/libexec/check_procs -w 01 -c 02 --metric=CPU
CPU CRITICAL: 1 crit, 0 warn out of 163 processes
```

Apply The Plug-in to A Device

Now that we know how to run our plug-in and know what to expect, we can log into Zenoss and edit the performance template for the target device. If we wanted to apply the plug-in to all devices in a class, we would either modify the device template for the class or create a new template and bind it to the class like we did in the HttpMonitor ZenPack example. For this example, however, we'll apply the plug-in at the individual device level.

Let's configure a new data source for our Zenoss server Fox:

1. From Fox's status page, select **More > Templates** from the page menu.
2. Click the Create Local Copy button for the device template.
3. Edit the Device template.
4. From the Data Source table menu, select Add Data Source.

5. In the Add a New Data Source dialog box, enter the following values:
    ◦ ID: checkCpu
    ◦ Type: Command

6. Click OK to add the data source and edit its properties.

7. Configure and save the data source as needed.

How we configure our data source depends on our individual setups (refer to the next screen capture). We'll take a moment to review the available properties and then come back to enter specific values.

Property	Description
Name	The name of the data source we enter in the Add a New Data Source dialog box.
Enabled	Set to **True** to enable the command.
Use SSH	Set to **False** to run the command only on the Zenoss server. Set to true to run the command on a remote server via SSH.
Component	Enter a descriptive component name to describe the event. Blank by default.
Event Class	Select the event class that this command should map to.
Event Key	Enter a descriptive event key to aid in event mappings. Blank by default.
Severity	Select a fail severity. Default is **Warning**.
Cycle Time	The time in seconds that Zenoss runs the command on the devices. The default is **300**.
Command Template	Specify the command to run the plug-in. Accepts TALES expressions that allows us to make the command generic for all devices in a class.

In our check_procs example, we can enter the command we tested into the Command Template box. However, if our command uses arguments such as device name or file system components, we could substitute absolute values by using TALES expressions, thereby making the command work regardless of the device.

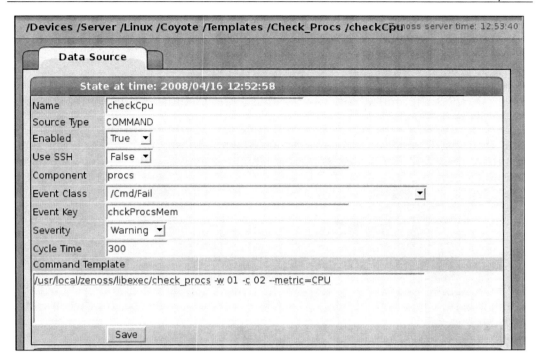

For example, if we want to monitor all the devices in a class with the check_disk plug-in, our command might look like:

```
/usr/local/zenoss/libexec/check_disk -w 5% -c 3% -p ${dev/compname}
```

In this case, the -p option specifies the partition name. By substituting the TALES expression for a partition name, the command becomes generic enough to run against all the devices.

When we specify the command, we may specify either the absolute path or just use the command name. If we do not specify the absolute path for the command, Zenoss uses the command path specified in the zCommandPath zProperty for the device. To eliminate a point of failure from our configuration, we will specify the absolute path in the Command Template.

Debug

After we add the new data source to our device, we need to make sure that it will run within Zenoss. We'll use two Zenoss commands: zentestcommand and zencommand. When we run zentestcommand, we should get the same output that we got when we ran the plug-in from the command line in 'Test the Plug-in' section. We run zencommand to provide a debugging output.

We supply zentestcommand the device name and the data source. The data source corresponds to the value we created in the previous section, 'Apply the Plug-in to a Device'. As the user zenoss, run the following command:

```
zentestcommand --device=Fox –datasource=checkCpu
```

The output of the command that we specified in the Command Template of the data source prints to the terminal.

After we verify that our new data source runs properly, we can test our plugin using the zencommand on the device. The zencommand daemon is responsible for running our commands.

```
zencommand run --device=Fox -v10
```

The -v10 option provides verbose output that we can use to validate that our command runs correctly. When we run zencommand from the command line, we mimic what Zenoss does when it monitors the device. We're looking for key pieces of information in the output. First, zencommand runs the plug-in command and prints the output. Second, we see an informational message which tells us how many commands are scheduled for the device. At this point, we expect to see this line in the output:

```
INFO: zen.zencommand:---------- - schedule has 1 command
```

This message confirms that our plug-in will run based on the cycle time interval we specify in the data source properties.

To illustrate an event, we set the CPU usage thresholds for the check_procs plug-in extremely low (1% for warning and 2%). When we check the **Events** tab for Fox, we see an event that was generated from zencommand.

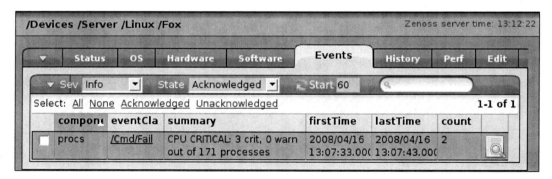

We need to take a moment to discuss how Zenoss translates a plug-in's warning and critical severities. If the plug-in returns a warning severity, Zenoss maps the event to the severity defined in the data source's properties. If the plug-in returns a critical severity, Zenoss maps the event to the next higher severity.

Zenoss Plugins

We installed the Zenoss plug-ins (`zenplugin.py`) on a remote machine in Chapter 5 and modeled a device using `zenplugin.py`. The following screenshot shows the file system template for the /Server/Cmd device class, which is using the disk collector plug-in. We note that the data **Source Type** is command and it's monitoring over SSH.

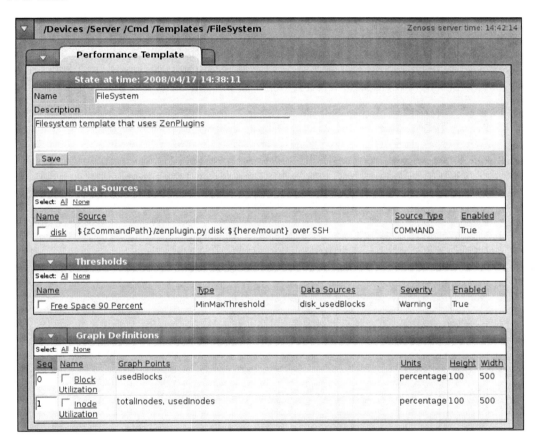

If we navigate to the Devices template for the /Server/Cmd device class, we can see examples using the mem, proc, and cpu collector plug-ins. We can configure the Zenoss Plug-ins in the same way in which we configured our Nagios plug-in check_procs.

Email Reports

Zenoss includes the `reportmail` command in `$ZENHOME/bin` that enables us to send an individual report via email. No graphical interface is available, which means that we must work from the command line as the Zenoss user.

We need to specify the URL of the report, the user name and the password for a Zenoss user, and the from address. Run the command `reportmail --help` to get a full list of options.

To get the URL of the report, we open the report we want to mail from the Zenoss UI, and copy the URL from our browser. For our example, we'll send the Device Changes Report to the Zenoss user mike, using the following command:

```
reportmail -u http://localhost:8080/zport/dmd/Reports/Device%20Reports/
Device%20Changes -U mike -p pass123 -f mike@badgerfiles.com
```

The command sends the Device Changes Report to the email address specified in the user settings for mike (refer to the following screenshot). The from address on the email is `mike@badgerfiles.com`. If we want to send the report to more than one email address, we include the `-a` option along with the additional email address. See the help file for more information.

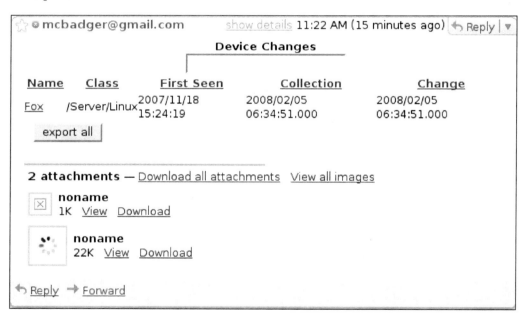

If we want to email the report out on a recurring basis, we can schedule it as a cron job. We talked about setting up cron jobs in the Automate Backups section of Chapter 9, and as a part of that section, we created a zenoss daily script in the `/home/zenoss/bin` directory. Then, we scheduled our script to run via crontab. As the Zenoss user, edit `zenoss_daily` and add our reportmail command. Our new script now looks like:

```
#!/bin/bash

# This script contains a short list of Zenoss commands that
# we want to run daily via cron.

#Setup Zenoss environment
export ZENHOME=/usr/local/zenoss
export PYTHONPATH=$ZENHOME/lib/python
export PATH=$ZENHOME/bin:$PATH

# Back up Zenoss and capture the verbose stdout to a log
zenbackup -v > $HOME\zenoss_daily.log

# Email Device Changes report.
reportmail -u http://localhost:8080/zport/dmd/Reports/
Device%20Reports/Device%20Changes -U mike -p pass123 -f mike@
badgerfiles.com

# end script
```

Our script poses a slight security risk in that we need to supply the user name and the password for a Zenoss account in order for the reportmail to work. We can take a few precautions with the user account we use with reportmail.

We should change the permissions on our `zenoss_daily` script so that only the Zenoss user can read it. From the `/home/zenoss/bin` directory, run the following command:

chmod 700 zenoss_daily

The user account should not match a user account on the host system, and the Zenoss account we use with reportmail should be set up with a ZenUser role within Zenoss.

Email Events

Turn email into events with zenmail and zenpop3. Zenmail allows us to start an internal SMTP server and direct other devices to send alerts directly to Zenoss via the open SMTP port. The message gets turned into an event in Zenoss. We can use the zenpop3 daemon to retrieve emails from a specified account and generate events based on those emails.

To use either program in daemon mode, we edit the $ZENHOME/bin/zenoss
configuration file, so that the daemons start when Zenoss starts. Also, the daemons
will be available via Settings > Daemons in the Zenoss portal.

As the Zenoss user:

1. Back up $ZENHOME/bin/zenoss.

2. Open $ZENHOME/bin/zenoss in a text editor.

3. Find the line in the script that begins with $ZENHOME/bin/zenfunctions and
   uncomment or add the following lines (refer to the next screenshot):

   ○ **C="$C zenmail"**

   ○ **C="$C zenpop3"**

4. Restart the Zenoss daemons with the command zenoss restart.

When we restart the Zenoss daemon, zenmail and zenpop3 print warning messages that tell us that they were unable to find the configuration files in /usr/local/zenoss/etc/. To clear those messages up, run the following commands as the Zenoss user:

```
zenmail genconf
zenpop3 genconf
```

The genconf option creates a configuration file in $ZENHOME/etc with all the available options for the daemon. Each Zenoss daemon accepts the genconf option. Now we're ready to configure zenmail and zenpop3.

Zenmail

The zenmail command is helpful because we can configure our devices to send email directly to the SMTP server running via zenmail. Zenoss turns the email into an event.

We do not use zenmail to send alert notifications to our users. Notifications are handled via the server we define on the Settings page in Zenoss. If we would try to configure the SMTP settings to use zenmail, any emails Zenoss sends to our users will end up in the Event Console, not our user's inbox.

If we want to bind the SMTP server to a port other than 25, we can edit the zenmail configuration file and add the parameter listenport followed by the new port number. We introduce the daemons and their configuration files in Chapter 9.

For a list of all options of zenmail, run the command:

```
zenmail --help
```

Zenpop3

In order to make zenpop3 work, we need to specify the mail server, user name, and password at a minimum:

1. In Zenoss, navigate to **Settings > Daemons**.
2. Edit the configuration for zenpop3.
3. Enter the following parameters followed by the correct POP3 server values (refer to the next screen capture):
   - pophost
   - popuser
   - poppass
   - cycletime

4. Save the configuration.

5. Restart zenpop3.

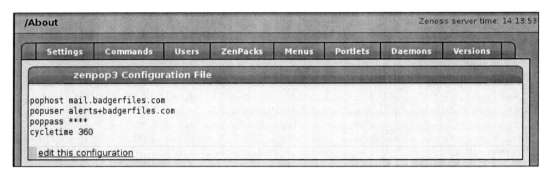

To test the setup, we send an email to the account we specified in the zenpop3 configuration. If everything is successful, we get an unknown event in the **Event Console** (refer to the following screenshot).

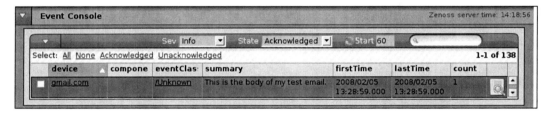

Now that we have the event, we can map it and process it in a way that meets our individual needs. Consult Chapter 7 for assistance on mapping and processing events.

Access Zenoss Objects Database with zendmd

Zenoss provides a Python shell called zendmd that allows us to access the Zenoss object database. From zendmd, we can write and test Python statements that manipulate the Zenoss objects. This section introduces the environment and provides some basic commands to get us started.

To start the zendmd shell, run the following command:

```
zendmd
```

The Zenoss dmd command shell opens and displays with a `>>>` prompt. Enter the following statements at the shell (exclude the commented text that begins with #):

```
zhelp()                 # Display a list of objects
dir(dmd)                # Display methods available to dmd object
dir(devices)    # Display methods available to devices object
find('Coyote')          # Find the device by name
d = find('Coyote')      # Assign the device to the variable d
d.deviceClass()  # Display the device class
```

The dmd object is the root of the Zenoss object database. When we execute the `dir(devices)` statement, one of the methods we return is `deviceClass()`, which we then use to print Coyote's device class. In this example, `d.deviceClass()` returns:

```
<DeviceClass at /zport/dmd/Devices/Server/Remote/devices/Coyote/
deviceClass/Remote>
```

The following script prints all the devices in the Zenoss object database with the corresponding device class. The zendmd command prompts are preserved:

```
>>> for x in dmd.Devices.getSubDevices():
...     print "%s, %s" % (x. x.getDeviceClassName())
...
```

When working in the zendmd shell, the line spacing of our code is important. Each line after line 1 is indented. The shell will print an indentation error message if we forget to indent. When we finish typing our python statement, hit enter on a blank line that's preceded by three periods (...) and the shell will evaluate the statement. Our sample script produces the following output:

```
<Device at Crow>, /Network/Router
<Device at Fox>, /Server/Linux
<Device at Master>, /Server/Windows
<Device at Coyote>, /Server/Remote
<Device at Print Server>, /Printer
<Device at Bobcat>, /Workstation
<Device at badgerfiles.com>, /Web
```

If we want to print only the devices in the /Server device class, our Python statement becomes:

```
>>>  for x in dmd.Devices.Server.getSubDevices():
...             print "%s, %s" % (x,  x.deviceClass())
...
```

If we want to print only the devices in the /Server/Linux device class, our Python statement becomes:

```
>>>   for x in dmd.Devices.Server.Linux.getSubDevices():
...            print "%s, %s" % (x,  x.deviceClass())
...
```

As we run each statement, our results become very specific. We can also commit changes to the Zenoss object database from zendmd. Our next example finds the device named Bobcat and sets the production state to Production.

```
>>> x = find('Bobcat')
...          x.productionState = 1000
....
>>> commit()
```

The commit() method applies our changes to the Zenoss object database. We can log into the Zenoss UI and verify if our statement executed correctly.

Summary

We've seen an overview of several ways in which we can extend the base functionality of Zenoss. However, we're not able to demonstrate all the configuration options and scenarios possible. The real enlightenment comes when each of us deploys Zenoss in our individual environments and finds creative ways to use ZenPacks, plug-ins, and email to manage our IT assets.

This chapter provides ample opportunity to make mistakes in our configuration, which means that we'll need to troubleshoot problems. The next Chapter outlines the tools we can use to troubleshoot and request support.

11
Technical Support

Despite our best efforts, we sometimes encounter problems with the software we use. As IT professionals, we accept this fate. Let's review some basic Zenoss troubleshooting and support options to help us identify and get answers to our problems.

Troubleshoot Zenoss

Zenoss provides several default options to help us identify and diagnose problems, including reports, log files, and Zenoss commands.

Reports

Zenoss includes several default reports that we can analyze to find potential problems with our monitoring setup. We reviewed each of the reports in detail in Chapter 8. The following table lists a problem description and the report that may provide the necessary information.

Problem	Report Name	Description
User is not alerted when an event occurs	Notification Schedules	Review the active notification window and filter rule for each user.
Device model does not update	Model Collection Age	Devices listed have not been monitored by SNMP for 48 hours.
SNMP monitoring problems	SNMP Status Issues	System wide view of all devices with SNMP issues by device class. Includes devices not monitored with SNMP.

Problem	Report Name	Description
Availability monitoring problems	Ping Status Issues	System wide view of all devices with ping issues by device class. Includes devices not monitored with ping.
Need to know available disk space across all devices on the network	Filesystem Utilization	All monitored file systems display in a single view.
Need to know the total network utilization for memory, CPU, and throughput	Aggregate Reports	All usages statistics for all monitored devices display in a single graph for each item.

Each report tells us something about the IT assets we monitor, which makes them valuable resources when we try to track down trends or problems.

Zenoss Daemons

Until now, we have been primarily interacting with the Zenoss daemons through the web interface. Now it's time to take a look under the hood at the daemons and see how they can aid our troubleshooting.

Before we jump into the command line debugging and log files, let's get a basic understanding of what each daemon does.

Daemon	Function
zenping	Monitors availability with ping.
zensyslog	Turns *nix based syslogs into events.
zenstatus	Monitors components with status monitors.
zenactions	Performs commands based on events. Event commands are user defined.
zentrap	Monitors SNMP traps.
zenmodeler	Models each device according to associated plugins.
zenperfsnmp	Collects performance data for components via SNMP.
zencommand	Runs external commands, such as Nagios plugins.
zenprocess	Collects SNMP performance data for CPU and Memory.
zenwin	Monitors WMI services on Windows systems.
zeneventlog	Monitors Windows event logs.
zenwinmodeler	Models Windows systems.

Basic Usage

All these daemons work in a consistent way in that they run in the background in daemon mode or in the foreground for debugging purposes. Consequently, we have two separate help files which we can review. We'll demonstrate using zenactions.

To see the daemon run options, use the command:

`zenactions --help`

The following screenshot shows the command's output:

```
zenoss@fox:~$ zenactions --help
Usage: /usr/local/zenoss/bin/zenactions {run|start|stop|restart|status|help|genconf} [options]

  where the commands are:

    run     - start the program but don't put it in the background.
              NB: This mode is good for debugging.

    start   - start the program in daemon mode -- running in the background,
              detached from the shell

    stop    - stop the program

    restart - stop and then start the program
              NB: Sometimes the start command will run before the daemon
                  has terminated.  If this happens just re-run the command.

    status  - Check the status of a daemon.  This will print the current
              process nuber if it is running.

    help    - display the options available for the daemon

    genconf - create an example configuration file with default settings

zenoss@fox:~$
```

To see the available options, run the command:

`zenactions help`

The following screen shot shows the options available to zenactions.

```
zenoss@fox:~$ zenactions help
usage: zenactions.py [options]

options:
  --version             show program's version number and exit
  -h, --help            show this help message and exit
  -v LOGSEVERITY, --logseverity=LOGSEVERITY
                        Logging severity threshold
  --logpath=LOGPATH     override default logging path
  -C CONFIGFILE, --configfile=CONFIGFILE
                        config file must define all params (see man)
  --uid=UID             user to become when running default:zenoss
  -c, --cycle           Cycle continuously on cycleInterval from zope
  -D, --daemon          Become a unix daemon
  --weblog              output log info in html table format
  --host=HOST           hostname of zeo server
  --port=PORT           port of zeo server
  -R DATAROOT, --dataroot=DATAROOT
                        root object for data load (i.e. /zport/dmd)
  --cachesize=CACHESIZE
                        in memory cachesize default: 1000
  --pcachename=PCACHENAME
                        persistent cache file name default:None
  --pcachedir=PCACHEDIR
                        persistent cache file directory
  --pcachesize=PCACHESIZE
                        persistent cache file size in MB
  --cycletime=CYCLETIME
                        check events every cycletime seconds
  --zopeurl=ZOPEURL     http path to the root of the zope server
  --genconf             Generate a template configuration file
  --genxmltable         Generate a Docbook table showing command-line
                        switches.
zenoss@fox:~$
```

The options available to the daemon vary based on the command. For example, some daemons allow us to specify a device, while others do not. However, each daemon allows us to specify the integer value of the level of logging we want to see.

The available logging levels from the least to most verbose are:

Log Severity	Numeric Value
Critical	50
Error	40
Info	20
Debug	10
Trace	5

Many of the daemons are set to log everything with a severity equal to or greater than info. However, when we're troubleshooting, we most likely want the verbose output provided by debug. If we are trying to isolate a command failure, we may need to specify a logging level of trace.

As the Zenoss user, run the following commands. Compare the output of these two commands:

```
zenstatus run
```

```
zenstatus run -v10
```

As we see, setting the logging level to debug creates a verbose output compared to the default level of info.

Note the syntax of our zenstatus examples. We supply `zenstatus` a command. In this case, we have provided `run`. Then we append the options we want to use. Our examples use the `logseverity` option. As an example, if we want to generate a sample configuration file using the default options, we supply the `genconf` command to the daemon, and the command looks like:

```
zenstatus genconf
```

The same rules apply to all the daemons.

Log Files

Each of the Zenoss daemons logs status messages to corresponding log files that we find in `$ZENHOME/logs`. We can also access the logs for each daemon by navigating to the Settings > Daemons page via the web interface.

Reviewing log files will help us confirm that Zenoss completes certain tasks. For example, if we need to troubleshoot the modeling process for a Windows server, we look through the `zenwinmodeler` log file to identify potential problems (see the following screen capture).

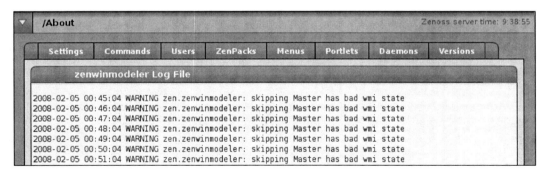

As we look through some of the log files, we may notice that the output for some of the daemons is more verbose than others. If we want to adjust the default logging level of the daemons, we can edit the configuration file and specify the logging level by specifying the parameter logseverity and the applicable value (see the following screenshot).

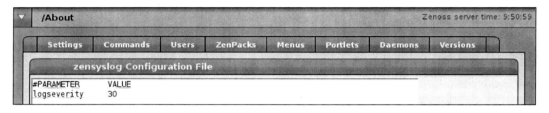

Community Support

For support, we turn to the Zenoss community at http://www.zenoss.com/ community/ for documentation, code, and discussion.

Documentation

The documentation contains a mix of community-contributed and company-sponsored documentation on a variety of topics. Our focus in this book has been fairly narrow in that we concentrate on setting up a monitoring environment from the web interface. The documentation is a great place to find advanced topics and development topics that provide a complementary perspective to the information in this book.

Code

Developers have not figured out how to write perfect code that works in all situations, so we expect to encounter software bugs as we use Zenoss. We don't want to expend energy troubleshooting known software issues. If we try something in Zenoss and it continues to fail even though we're sure we've done everything correctly, search the current bug tickets in Trac, Zenoss' incident tracker.

Discuss

At some point, we will need to ask questions to the Zenoss community via one of several mediums: IRC, mailing lists, and forums.

To interact with other community members in real time, we can use IRC. Connect to:

- Server: irc.freenode.net port 6667
- Channel: #zenoss

The mailing lists and forums are synchronized, so we can subscribe to the email list or browse the forums based on our individual preferences. The following groups exist:

- Zenoss Users: Main support forum for help with installation, configuration, and use.
- Zenoss ZenPack: Help with the development and distribution of ZenPacks.
- Zenoss Dev: A resource for Zenoss developers.
- Zenoss Announce: Lists new releases and Zenoss announcements.

Remember, the forums are not for real-time discussions, and the people who respond are donating their time to help us.

Commercial Support

This book focuses on how to configure and use Zenoss Core to monitor our networks and systems. Zenoss Inc. provides a commercial version called Zenoss Enterprise that includes professional support subscriptions and enhanced software features.

Zenoss Enterprise includes the following default features:

- Global dashboard that aggregates data from multiple Zenoss installations.
- Synthetic transactions to test web, database, email, and performance.
- An advanced report library.
- Predictive threshold trending.
- Certified builds and ZenPacks.
- Integration with RANCID, Remedy, and LDAP.

For more information about Zenoss Enterprise, visit `http://www.zenoss.com/product/enterprise`.

Support Subscriptions

In addition to community support, Zenoss Inc. provides support subscriptions for both the core and enterprise editions of Zenoss. Organizations may choose from Core Support, Enterprise Silver, and Enterprise Gold subscriptions.

The core support option provides the same fully-functional software that we've covered in this book, but extends professional support to the organizations which need it. The enterprise support options include the enhanced Zenoss Enterprise software with additional support options and decreased incident response times.

For more information on the support offerings from Zenoss Inc., visit http://www.zenoss.com/product/overview#subscriptions.

Consulting

Need help customizing or deploying Zenoss? Zenoss Inc. provides consulting services to help organizations, and to plan, deploy, customize, and integrate a Zenoss monitoring solution into an organization.

For more information about consulting services, visit http://www.zenoss.com/product/#consulting.

Training

Zenoss Inc. provides a two-day, hands-on Zenoss administration course at the company's, headquarters at Annapolis, Maryland. The Zenoss Enterprise subscription plans include at least one training seat with the subscription.

Summary

Zenoss is a complex software package wrapped in an accessible web interface, which enables ready access to enterprise quality network and system monitors to the masses. As we gain familiarity with Zenoss through daily usage, our knowledge will grow, and we'll find ways to make Zenoss a better tool for our environments.

Zenoss is flexible enough to accommodate all skill levels. The user who never monitored anything gains value by having an easy to use interface while advanced users can probe deeper by manipulating Zenoss at the command and code levels.

For all users, the discovery begins at port 8080 of our Zenoss servers.

Event Attributes

Each Zenoss event includes several attributes to describe the details of an event; however, not all fields are populated for each event. The event fields defined in this table can be found in the log for an event, which is accessible from the Event Console. We can also configure our event views to display events using these fields via the Event Manager. We cover the Event Console and event views in Chapter 7.

The event fields are valid attributes that we can substitute in our Python statements via TALES expressions. Appendix B lists some of the device attributes that we can use with TALES.

Event Field	Description
dedupid	Identifies the event so that Zenoss can deduplicate events. Takes the form of device | component | eventClass | eventKey | severity.
evid	A unique identifier for the event.
device	Specifies the device attached to the event.
component	The Zenoss daemon reporting the event.
eventClass	The event class the event maps to.
eventKey	A user-defined way to map events. Event keys can be sequenced to aid the event class mapping of events from a common source to different event classes.
summary	Summary of the event.

Event Field	Description
message	Message body for the event. May be the same as summary.
severity	An Numeric representation of the event:
	5 = Critical
	4 = Error
	3 = Warning
	2 = Info
	1 = Debug
	0 = Clear
eventState	Numeric representation of the event state:
	0 = New
	1 = Acknowledged
	2 = Suppressed
eventClassKey	Maps the event to an event class.
eventGroup	Event source group: for example, syslog, Process, ping.
stateChange	Time stamp when the event state changed.
firstTime	Time stamp when the event first occurred.
lastTime	Time stamp when the event last occurred.
count	The total number of times the event has occurred based on the dedupid.
prodState	The production state of the device. The Zenoss defaults are:
	1000 = Production
	500 = Pre-Production
	Test = 400
	Maintenance = 300
	Decommissioned = -1
suppid	If the event is suppressed, this is the ID of the suppressing event.
manager	The fully qualified domain name of the event collector that generated the event.

Event Field	Description
agent	Reports the Zenoss daemon responsible for generating the event.
DeviceClass	The device class.
Location	The location organizer assigned to the device.
Systems	The system organizer assigned to the device.
DeviceGroups	The group organizer assigned to the device.
ipAddress	The IP address of the device.
facility	The syslog subsystem that generated the event (for example, cron, mail, lpr, auth, authpriv, daemon, ftp, kern, mark, news, syslog, user, uucp, local0 through local7).
priority	The priority of the syslog event.
ntevid	The Event ID field of the Windows NT event log.
ownerid	The ID number of the event owner.
clearid	The ID number of the event that cleared this event.
DevicePriority	The priority as assigned in the device's Edit page: 5 = Highest 4 = High 3 = Normal 2 = Low 1 = Lowest 0 = Trivial
eventClassMapping	The event class mapping used to evaluate and map the event.

B
TALES and Device Attributes

Throughout the book, we encounter many fields that accept TALES expressions including user commands, event commands, performance templates, zProperties, event mappings, and event transformations. Zenoss uses the Template Attribute Language Expression Syntax (TALES) to retrieve device and event attributes for Zenoss objects within any valid Python statement.

If we want to access device attributes, we use the syntax:

```
${device/attribute}
```

For example, Zenoss includes the following user command:

```
traceroute -q 1 -w 2 ${device/manageIp}
```

The TALES expression substitutes the device IP address that we normally expect to enter when we run the `traceroute` command manually. This makes sure that the same command can be run for any device and that the correct device IP will be substituted into the command.

If we want to access event attributes, we use the following syntax:

```
${evt/attribute}
```

For example, we create a custom event command in Chapter 7 to write some event information to a file:

```
echo "The Event with ID ${evt/evit} is on fire!"  >> /tmp/
SampleEventCommand
```

In this command, we use TALES to substitute the event ID. When the event runs, we get the following line in our file:

```
The Event with ID 7f000001365df722fffe960 is on fire!
```

The following table includes a list of the attributes that we may use when working with our devices. We can find many of these attributes on display on an individual device's Status page.

For a list of event specific attributes, see the list of event fields in Appendix A.

Device Attributes	Description
id	The device name, which is not necessarily the fully qualified domain name..
manageIp	The IP address of the device.
productionState	The numeric value of the device's production state: 1000 = Production 500 = Pre-Production 400 = Test 300 = Maintenance -1 = Decommissioned
productionStateString	The device's production state as a human-readable string.
priority	The numeric priority value: 5 = Highest 4 = High 3 = Normal 2 = Low 1 = Lowest 0 = Trivial
priorityString	The device's priority as a human-readable string.
locationName	The location organizer assigned to the device.
systemNames	The list of system organizers assigned to the device.
groupNames	The list of group organizers assigned to the device.
snmpDescr	The SNMP Description.
snmpOID	The OID from SNMP.
snmpContact	The SNMP contact value.

Device Attributes	Description
snmpSysName	The system name from SNMP.
snmpLastCollection	The last time Zenoss collected SNMP data for the device.
comments	User-entered comments on the device.
uptimeStr	The uptime values for the device.
pingStatusString	The device's ping status:
	0 = Up
	1 = Down
	2 = None
snmpStatusString	The device's SNMP status:
	0 = Up
	1 = Down
	2 = None.
osVersion	The operating system version .
osProductName	The software product name defined on the device's edit page.
osManufactureName	The operating system manufacturer name defined on the device's edit page.
hwProductName	The hardware product name defined on the device's edit page.
hwManufacturerName	The hardware manufacturer name defined on the device's edit page.

Index

monitors
about 97, 98
performance monitors 100, 101
status monitors 98
multi-graph reports
adding 173-178

N

Nagios plug-ins 224
navigation techniques, Zenoss
bread crumbs 46
navigation panel 44
table menus 46
tabs 46
network
adding 57, 58
zProperties 59
new devices report 165

O

Object Identifiers. *See* **OIDs**
OIDs 39
OS tab, component status
about 104
file systems 116, 117
interfaces 105-107
IP services 112-114
OS processes 107-110
routes 117, 118
services 110, 112
Win services 114, 115
OS tab, model devices 91

P

performance and availability, collection layer
performance daemon 21
zencommand, performance daemon 21
zenperfsnmp, performance daemon 21
zenping, performance daemon 21
zenprocess, performance daemon 21
zenstatus, performance daemon 21
performance daemon
zencommand 21

zenperfsnmp 21
zenping 21
zenprocess 21
zenstatus 21
performance graphs
about 118-120
performance monitors
about 13, 100, 101
config cycle interval 101
event log cycle interval 101
monitor, adding 102
monitor, attaching to devices 102-104
process cycle interval 101
render URL 101
render user 101
SNMP performance cycle interval 101
status cycle interval 101
windows modeler cycle interval 101
windows service cycle interval 101
performance reports
about 178
aggregate reports 178, 179
availability report 179, 180
CPU utilization 180, 181
filesystem utilization report 181, 182
interface utilization report 182
memory utilization report 182, 183
threshold summary 183, 184
performance templates
about 120, 121
data sources 122
graph definitions 124
thresholds 123
Perf tab 118, 119
ping status issues report 165
plug-ins
about 224
applying, to device 225-227
debugging 227-229
testing 224, 225
plug-ins, Zenoss 87
portlets, main views
about 47
adding 48
arranging 48
device issues portlet 49

status issues report 166
SNMP, model devices
collector plug-ins 83, 84
model device 84-90
port scan modeling 90
SSH collector plug-ins 86, 87
SSH modeling 86
testing 80-82
windows considerations 82, 83
Zenoss plug-ins 87
SNMP collector plug-ins 83, 84
SNPP
about 196
host 197
port 197
software inventory report 166, 167
software packages, prerequisites 27
source installation
system setup 33, 34
Ubuntu notes 32, 33
Zenoss, building 35
Zenoss, installing 35, 36
Zenoss source, downloading 34
SSH collector plug-ins 86
SSH modeling 86
status monitors
about 98
chunk size 99
configuration 98
configuration reload interval 99
cycle interval 99
maximum failures 99
monitor name 99
ping timeout 99
ping tries 99
syslog messages
cisco router syslogs, collecting 129
forwarding, to Zenoss 129, 130
monitoring 127-129
syslog configuration testing, logger used
131
system reports 13

T

TALES
about 249

Template Attribute Language Expression
Syntax. *See* TALES
thresholds, performance templates
about 123
customizing 125
**threshold summary, performance reports
183, 184**
troubleshooting, Zenoss
about 237
reports 237, 238

U

updating, Zenoss core 210, 211
user account, Zenoss
adding 47
user layer 16, 17
user management
about 185
administered objects 188, 189
event views, defining 189
event views, properties 190
users, assigning to groups 195, 196
user reports
notification schedules report 184

V

virtual appliance
advantages 27
installing 28, 29
working with 29-31
VMware player
downloading 28, 29
installing 28, 29

W

web portal 8
web site
monitoring, HttpMonitor used 216-221
windows event logs, monitoring
about 131, 132
event log configuration, testing with
Eventcreate 132
Windows Management Instrumentation.
See WMI

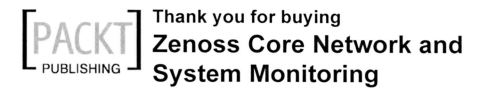

Thank you for buying
Zenoss Core Network and System Monitoring

Packt Open Source Project Royalties

When we sell a book written on an Open Source project, we pay a royalty directly to that project. Therefore by purchasing Zenoss Core Network and System Monitoring, Packt will have given some of the money received to the Zenoss project.

In the long term, we see ourselves and you—customers and readers of our books—as part of the Open Source ecosystem, providing sustainable revenue for the projects we publish on. Our aim at Packt is to establish publishing royalties as an essential part of the service and support a business model that sustains Open Source.

If you're working with an Open Source project that you would like us to publish on, and subsequently pay royalties to, please get in touch with us.

Writing for Packt

We welcome all inquiries from people who are interested in authoring. Book proposals should be sent to authors@packtpub.com. If your book idea is still at an early stage and you would like to discuss it first before writing a formal book proposal, contact us; one of our commissioning editors will get in touch with you.

We're not just looking for published authors; if you have strong technical skills but no writing experience, our experienced editors can help you develop a writing career, or simply get some additional reward for your expertise.

About Packt Publishing

Packt, pronounced 'packed', published its first book "Mastering phpMyAdmin for Effective MySQL Management" in April 2004 and subsequently continued to specialize in publishing highly focused books on specific technologies and solutions.

Our books and publications share the experiences of your fellow IT professionals in adapting and customizing today's systems, applications, and frameworks. Our solution-based books give you the knowledge and power to customize the software and technologies you're using to get the job done. Packt books are more specific and less general than the IT books you have seen in the past. Our unique business model allows us to bring you more focused information, giving you more of what you need to know, and less of what you don't.

Packt is a modern, yet unique publishing company, which focuses on producing quality, cutting-edge books for communities of developers, administrators, and newbies alike. For more information, please visit our website: www.PacktPub.com.

Configuring IPCop Firewalls

ISBN: 1-904811-36-1   Paperback: 154 pages

How to setup, configure and manage your Linux firewall, web proxy, DHCP, DNS, time server, and VPN with this powerful Open Source solution

1. Learn how to install, configure, and set up IPCop on your Linux servers

2. Use IPCop as a web proxy, DHCP, DNS, time server, and VPN

3. Advanced add-on management

Linux Thin Client Networks Design and Deployment

ISBN: 978-1-847192-04-2   Paperback: 180 pages

A quick guide for System Administrators

1. Learn to implement the right Linux thin client network for your requirements

2. Evaluate and choose the right hardware and software for your deployment

3. Techniques to intelligently design and set up your thin client network

4. Practical advice on educating users, convincing management, and intelligent use of legacy systems

Please check **www.PacktPub.com** for information on our titles

PUBLISHING

Designing and Implementing
Linux Firewalls and QoS
using netfilter, iproute2, NAT, and L7-filter

Learn how to secure your system and implement QoS
using real-world scenarios for networks of all sizes

Lucian Gheorghe

PACKT

Designing and Implementing Linux Firewalls and QoS using netfilter, iproute2, NAT and l7-filter

ISBN: 1-904811-65-5   Paperback: 280 pages

Learn how to secure your system and implement QoS
using real-world scenarios for networks of all sizes

1. Implementing Packet filtering, NAT,
   bandwidth shaping, packet prioritization
   using netfilter/iptables, iproute2, Class Based
   Queuing (CBQ) and Hierarchical Token
   Bucket (HTB)

2. Designing and implementing 5 real-world
   firewalls and QoS scenarios ranging from small
   SOHO offices to a large scale ISP network that
   spans many cities

3. Building intelligent networks by marking,
   queuing, and prioritizing different types
   of traffic

SSL VPN
Understanding, evaluating, and planning secure,
web-based remote access

Joseph Steinberg   Tim Speed

PACKT

SSL VPN

ISBN: 1-904811-07-8   Paperback: 194 pages

A comprehensive overview of SSL VPN technologies
and design strategies

1. Understand how SSL VPN technology works

2. Evaluate how SSL VPN could fit into your
   organisation?s security strategy

3. Practical advice on educating users, integrating
   legacy systems, and eliminating security
   loopholes

3. Written by experienced SSL VPN and data
   security professionals

Please check **www.PacktPub.com** for information on our titles

Printed in the United States
117680LV00002B/50/P